Words for Students of English

Vocabulary Series Editors
Holly Deemer Rogerson
Lionel Menasche

WORDS
for Students of English

A Vocabulary Series for ESL

Holly Deemer Rogerson
Gary Esarey
Linda M. Schmandt
Dorolyn A. Smith

Pitt Series in English as a Second Language

Ann Arbor
University of Michigan Press

First published by the University of Michigan Press 1993
Copyright © 1988, University of Pittsburgh Press and
   the English Language Institute, University of Pittsburgh
All rights reserved
ISBN 0-472-08212-4
Published in the United States of America by
The University of Michigan Press
Manufactured in the United States of America

2005   2004   2003   2002   10   9   8   7

Illustrations by Suzanne T. Hershelman

Contents

Foreword

The objective of this series of vocabulary texts for the student of English as a foreign language is to facilitate the learning of approximately 3,000 new base words. Vocabulary learning has long been deemphasized in language teaching, much to the detriment of the students, who have mostly been left to fend for themselves. We thoroughly agree with Muriel Saville-Troike, who states, "Vocabulary knowledge in English is the most important aspect of oral English proficiency for academic achievement" (*TESOL Quarterly*, vol. 18, no. 2, p. 216).

With the present lack of comprehensive vocabulary texts suitable for both classroom use and home study, this series is intended to support teachers in preparing effective vocabulary lessons so that they can meet their students' urgent need for an increased lexicon. We present here a selection of base vocabulary items and some of their derived forms (i.e., the noun, verb, adverb, and adjective of the same stem) together with a series of exercises designed to help students remember the new words and use them in context.

This text has been used in an experimental edition in the English Language Institute, and modifications suggested by its use have been incorporated in the present version.

Christina Bratt Paulston
Director, English Language Institute
University of Pittsburgh

Acknowledgments

A series such as this depends greatly on the cooperation and hard work of numerous people:

Christina Bratt Paulston and Holly Deemer Rogerson originated the idea for the series.

Christina Bratt Paulston provided ongoing support for the series.

Mary Newton Bruder, Carol Jasnow, Christina Bratt Paulston, and Holly Deemer Rogerson developed the first version of the list of approximately 600 words assumed known.

Holly Deemer Rogerson developed the original pool of words from which the 150 topic word lists were chosen. She also organized the word lists and provided general management of the project, including authors' drafts, revisions, editing, illustrations, duplicating, testing, and typing.

Ideas for word lists, format, and exercise types were contributed by Betsy Davis, Gary Esarey, Suzanne T. Hershelman, Carol Jasnow, Carol Moltz, Lionel Menasche, Holly Deemer Rogerson, Dorolyn Smith, and Linda M. Schmandt.

Final revisions of content were done by Lionel Menasche and Holly Deemer Rogerson, with input from classroom testing by Isabel Dillener, Caroline Haessly, Pat Furey, Carol Jasnow, Linda M. Schmandt, Jill Sherman, and Tom Swinscoe.

JoEllen Walker typed several drafts of the manuscript.

Lisa Krizmanich assisted during the testing phase.

Introduction

Volumes 1–6 of *Words for Students of English*, each containing 25 units, present English base words,* with definitions, examples, and exercises. The texts may be used as core texts for vocabulary learning classes or as supplementary texts in reading, speaking, and writing classes. They may also be used for individual study.

Each unit focuses on one topic so that the words being presented can be practiced in meaningful contexts. Some of the new words in each unit are directly related to the topic, while others are less directly connected. Most of the words in a given unit can be used in a variety of contexts.

Volume 1 assumes a knowledge of 600 base words in English. Starting from this point, new words are presented in each unit, with the definitions, examples, and exercises *containing only vocabulary which has been previously learned.* The first units in Volume 1 contain only about ten base words each in order to allow the students to become familiar with the format of the units. After the first units, each unit in Volume 1 contains approximately fifteen base words. In Volume 2, there are approximately fifteen base words in each unit. In Volumes 3 and 4, each unit contains fifteen to twenty base words, and, in Volumes 5 and 6, there are approximately 25 base words per unit. On completion of the series of six volumes, students will have learned approximately 3,000 base words.

Given that Volume 1 assumes a knowledge of 600 base words, the level of Volumes 1 and 2 can be loosely described as beginning, Volumes 3 and 4 as intermediate, and Volumes 5 and 6 as high intermediate or advanced.

---

*"Base" may be defined variously in lexical analysis, but for our present pedagogical purpose it implies any alternant from which other forms are derived. It is frequently impossible to say which form of a word is the most basic.

Selection of Words and Unit Topics

The 600 assumed words upon which Volumes 1–6 are based were chosen by a panel of experienced ESL teachers at the University of Pittsburgh as the group of words which are most typically learned by ESL students during their first two years of middle school or high school ESL classes. The words presented in Volumes 1–6 were selected according to usefulness from a variety of word-frequency lists. The authors and editors added other words to the topics at suitable levels of difficulty.

In many cases students have to learn words with more than one meaning or with meanings that may vary according to context. A decision was made in each such instance as to whether the meaning in the new context was different enough to warrant further definition or similar enough for the students to extrapolate from what they had previously learned. These decisions were based on dictionary definitions and authors' or editors' personal judgments. For example, a word such as *beat* might appear in these contexts: (a) beat the opposing football team, (b) beat a drum, (c) a beat of a heart, (d) beat a person. Contexts (b) and (d) (meaning = strike) were judged close enough to allow extrapolation of meaning from one context to another, but (a) and (c) were thought to require separate definitions.

We have assumed that when a student learns a new vocabulary item, an approximate meaning for the word is assimilated, and that meaning is linked to the context in which the word was first encountered. Then, as the student meets the word in other contexts, the initially learned, approximate meaning is expanded and refined. Hence, many words are not only used several times in the unit in which they first appear, but are also used in later units.

The unit topics were chosen and ordered according to their perceived relevance to the students' lives, that is, their communicative usefulness. Most topics are covered in one unit in each volume, but certain broad topics, for example "School," are repeated twice within the same volume, in which case they are marked (A) or (B). A few topics, such as "Religion" and "Banking," due to the difficulty or abstractness of the words associated with them, are not covered in the first volume. Certain other topics whose words were perceived as tangible and easy, for example, "Telephone" and "Post Office," are completed in the first two volumes.

It should be noted that the repetition of each topic, at times within the same volume and always in at least one subsequent volume, allows for review and recycling of the material learned. Thus, long-term retention of the vocabulary is facilitated.

Format and Suggestions for Teachers

Flexibility in using this vocabulary series has been a prime consideration in planning the format and exercises of the units. Therefore, although suggestions are given in the following paragraphs, it is assumed that teachers in different situations will decide according to their own students' needs whether work should be done in or out of class, orally or in writing, and with or without direct assistance from the teacher. The pace at which classes can proceed through each volume will vary greatly, depending on the students' motivation, study habits, and general workload, as well as the degree of emphasis the teacher wishes to place on productive vocabulary skills.

Each unit in Volumes 1–6 has the same format. The five sections of each unit are as follows.

WORD FORM CHART
DEFINITIONS AND EXAMPLES
INTRODUCTORY EXERCISES
STUDY EXERCISES
FOLLOW-UP

The WORD FORM CHART presents base words and some or all of their related forms, categorized by part of speech. In Volumes 1 and 2, an effort was made to simplify the charts by omitting many derived or related forms which were either not common, or not useful for students at this level, or not easily recognizable from a knowledge of the base form. After Volume 2, more related forms are added because the students can handle more as they progress in learning the language. Decisions on what forms to omit were made by authors and editors on the basis of experience gained during testing of these materials with linguistically heterogeneous classes. Teachers in different educational contexts should consider supplementing the charts according to their own students' needs and their ability to absorb more material. For example, many words could be added by giving antonyms formed from words already given (planned/unplanned, honest/dishonest).

In the NOUNS column of the charts in Volumes 1 and 2 only, nouns which normally or frequently refer to humans are marked by the symbol ⚥. When a noun, as defined in the unit, can be either human or nonhuman, the symbol is in parentheses: (⚥). Gerunds are not included in the charts. Nouns have not been marked "count" and "non-count" because so many nouns function in both ways.

In the VERBS column, irregular past tenses and past participles are in parentheses following the verbs. In cases where more than one past tense or past participle is acceptable, the more regular one is included in the chart. Thus, for example, in the Volume 1, Unit #4 Word Form Chart no irregular forms are listed for *forecast* because the regular form *forecasted* is also currently acceptable.

In the ADJECTIVES column, we have included any present or past participles that appear prenominally as adjectives, as well as any regular adjectives. We have not included in this column nouns which form Noun-Noun modification patterns.

The next section, DEFINITIONS AND EXAMPLES, gives the meanings of the words as well as example sentences which are usually related to the topic of the unit. The form chosen for definition is not always the base form. Other forms are sometimes chosen for greater ease of definition or learning. In all definitions and examples, only previously learned words are used. This applies also within the set of definitions in each unit. Thus, the words in each set of definitions are presented in an order which allows their definition and exemplification using only previously introduced words. Grammatical information is given in the definitions by means of the following conventions: "to" is used before a verb to indicate the verb form, articles are used with nouns whenever possible to indicate that the word is a noun, and parentheses enclose prepositions that may follow a verb. Words with more than one meaning are cross-referenced to definitions in earlier units when new definitions are given. This section, together with the Word Form Chart, can be efficiently handled as work assigned for intensive individual study, followed by discussion in class of questions raised by students. At this point the teacher may also wish to elaborate on certain definitions and give further examples.

Writing explicit definitions of words using the intentionally limited vocabulary available results in some rather broad definitions and others that are limited to certain aspects of the meaning. The deliberate compromise here between precision and generality is designed to make the text fully accessible to students by avoiding the major weakness of many other vocabulary texts: defining new items with words that are themselves unknown to the learner. The easily understood broad definitions, which may take the form of a standard verbal definition, a picture, or a list of examples, are then refined by further exposure to appropriate examples in this unit and series and in the students' later reading. Also, students can usefully refer to a bilingual dictionary in conjunction with studying the example sentences given.

After the Definitions and Examples section, there is a three-tiered system of exercises sequenced to take the student from easy, open-book, fairly controlled exercises through more difficult, less controlled exercises to a final phase with communicative exercises.

The first part of the sequence consists of INTRODUCTORY EXERCISES. These are designed to acquaint the students with the new words in the unit and lead them to an initial understanding of the words by using the Definitions and Examples section. We recommend that these brief and easy exercises be done with books open, orally or in writing, immediately after the teacher's first presentation of the new words.

The next section in each unit, headed STUDY EXERCISES, is a longer and more difficult set of exercises designed to be used by the students for individual study or for oral or written work in class.

The final section is the FOLLOW-UP. This includes a dictation and more open-ended communicative exercises designed to be done after the students have studied the words. The latter may be done orally in class, or teachers may request written answers to selected questions.

Each volume also contains an INDEX listing all the base words presented in that volume. Words in the preceding volumes are given in separate appendices. With each word is listed the volume and unit where it is presented. The 600 initially assumed words are also in an appendix.

An ANSWER KEY at the end of each volume provides answers for all the exercises in the Study Exercises sections, except where a variety of answers is acceptable. Answers are not provided for the Introductory Exercises or the exercises in the Follow-Up so that the teacher can choose to use these exercises for homework or testing purposes if desired.

Production and Recognition

Although a distinction between vocabulary known for recognition and that known for production is often propounded, the actual situation is probably best represented by a continuum stretching from mere recognition to production which is accurate both semantically and syntactically. The exercises in Volumes 1–6 cover the full range of this continuum so that teachers wishing to stress productive vocabulary knowledge will have ample opportunity to give their students feedback on the use of the new words in their speech and writing. However, the goal of many teachers will be to increase their students' recognition vocabularies as rapidly as possible, with the expectation that those words which students meet again frequently in other contexts and have a use for will gradually become part of their productive vocabularies. Teachers with this goal of recognition vocabulary development in mind will wish to proceed more rapidly through the units and deemphasize those exercises requiring productive capabilities, for example, by limiting their corrections to semantic errors, rather than correcting syntactic mistakes as well.

Words for Students of English

Education (A)

Word Form Chart

NOUN	VERB	ADJECTIVE	ADVERB
absence		absent	
advance	advance	advanced	
		advancing	
chalk		chalky	
	compel	compulsory	
education	educate	educated	
error			
example		exemplary	
failure	fail	failing	
level			
	miss	missing	
note	note		
	pass	passing	
		private	privately
		public	publicly
typewriter	type	typed	
		typing	
typist 人			

Definitions and Examples

1. **absent** [not in class]

   Students who are **absent** from class too often will not do well on examinations.

   A: Why were you **absent** yesterday?
   B: I was sick.

2. **advanced** [difficult, requiring a lot of skill; past the beginning]

   You can take the **advanced** course if you do well in the beginning course.

   A: How did you get into the **advanced** class?
   B: I'm good at languages.

3. **chalk** [what the teacher writes with on the blackboard, usually white]

   The teacher could not find any **chalk**.

   A: Will you run out and get me some **chalk**?
   B: Sure.

4. **educate** [to teach; to give schooling for a length of time]

   It is difficult and expensive to **educate** young people.

   A: Are your children going to be **educated** in English?
   B: No, in our language.

5. **compulsory** [required]

   Education is **compulsory** for young people.

   A: I don't want to take a foreign language.
   B: You have to. It's **compulsory**.

6. **note** [something written to help you remember; something short written to another person]

   Alfonso takes clear **notes** in all his classes.
   I wrote a thank-you **note** to Maria.

   A: I may forget to buy the book.
   B: Make a **note** of it. Then you won't forget.

7. **error** [a mistake]

   She made an **error** in her application.

   A: My professor wouldn't read my paper.
   B: Why not?
   A: It had too many careless **errors**.

8. **example** [one thing from a group, showing what the others are like]

   The teacher did one of the homework problems as an **example**.

   A: I didn't understand what you said.
   B: Let me give you an **example**.

9. **fail** [not to succeed in an examination or a course]

   If you **fail** the final exam, you will **fail** the course.

   A: I feel terrible. I **failed** the test.
   B: Try to do better on the next one.

10. **level** [a class or place decided by how much knowledge or skill you have]

    Some schools require an advanced **level** course in a language before you can graduate.

    A: What **level** of Spanish are you taking?
    B: Beginning.

11. **miss** (a) [to not go to class, work, a party, etc.]

    Because she **missed** too many classes, she failed the exam.
    If you **miss** many days of work, you may lose some pay.

    A: Why did you **miss** the party last night?
    B: I was sick.

    (b) [to answer incorrectly]

    If a student understands the lesson, he will not **miss** many answers on a test.

12. **pass** [to be successful in an exam or a course]

    All the students **passed** the final exam and **passed** the course.

13. **private** [not open to all people]

    Private schools may be very expensive because they do not receive much money from the government.

    A: Did you go to a **private** school?
    B: No. That was too expensive for my family.

14. **public** [open to all people]

    Tuition at **public** universities is cheaper than tuition at private universities.

    A: Is Ohio State University a **public** school?
    B: Yes.

15. **type** [to write with a machine]

   Every college student should know how to **type**.

   A: What's the problem with your paper?
   B: My professor won't read it because I didn't **type** it.

Introductory Exercises

A. Match each word with its definition.

_____ 1. to write with a machine

_____ 2. open to all people

_____ 3. to be unsuccessful in an exam

_____ 4. a mistake

_____ 5. something which your teacher writes with on the blackboard

_____ 6. difficult, requiring a lot of skill

_____ 7. to teach

_____ 8. not open to all people

_____ 9. to be successful in an exam or course

_____ 10. to answer incorrectly

a. absent
b. advanced
c. chalk
d. compulsory
e. educate
f. error
g. example
h. fail
i. level
j. miss
k. note
l. pass
m. private
n. public
o. type

B. Listen to the sentence. Say the related word from the word form chart.

1. The student does well on the exam.
2. The government pays for this school.
3. You use a machine to write.
4. You make a mistake.
5. This is a course that you have to take.
6. This is something white that the teacher writes with in the classroom.
7. The student goes to school for this.
8. This course is not for beginners.
9. The student is not in class today. (two answers)
10. You do not pass the course.
11. You send a very short letter written to someone.

Study Exercises

C. Write **T** if the sentence is true and **F** if it is false.

_____ **1.** Children may be educated in public or private schools in many countries.

_____ **2.** If you fail a course, you may have to take it again.

_____ **3.** Students in this class must type their assignments.

_____ **4.** Private universities are usually expensive.

_____ **5.** A student should know how to take good notes.

_____ **6.** The teacher may write an example with chalk.

_____ **7.** You should be absent often if you want to pass a course.

_____ **8.** In most countries education is compulsory for people who are older than eighteen.

_____ **9.** Students often use chalk to write their assignments.

_____ **10.** The advanced level course is difficult for beginners.

D. In the blanks, write the appropriate word(s) from the word form chart in this unit.

1. Young people go to school to be _____-d .

2. If you study hard, you should _____ the course.

3. In most countries, education is _____ for children.

4. If you make an _____ , try to correct it yourself.

5. Tuition is usually very expensive at _____ schools.

6. I feel I am ready for the advanced _____ course.

7. If you do well in the beginning piano class, you will be allowed to take _____ lessons.

8. The teacher gave me a low grade because I was _____ from class so many times.

9. Look at the end of the chapter. There are some _____-s that make it clear.

10. That professor requires all students to _____ their papers. You may not write your paper by hand.

11. It is a _____ school. The government pays for it.

E.   Synonyms and Antonyms

I. Write the letter of the word that has an opposite meaning.

____ **1.** error
____ **2.** fail
____ **3.** public
____ **4.** advanced
____ **5.** compulsory

a. level
b. chosen
c. pass
d. example
e. schedule
f. correction
g. private
h. beginning

II. Write the letter of the word that has a similar meaning.

____ **1.** error
____ **2.** educate
____ **3.** miss
____ **4.** note

a. course
b. be absent
c. grade
d. short letter
e. teach
f. mistake

F.   Read the passage and answer the questions that follow.

Education in the United States is compulsory for children up to about the age of sixteen. Most young people stay in school longer than that. Most graduate from high school at the age of seventeen or eighteen.

5   Almost half of these high school graduates continue their education at a college or university. Education for most young people in this country is free up to the time they graduate from high school. There are private schools, but most parents send their children to public schools, where

10   students do not pay tuition. When young people go to college, however, they must pay tuition at a public university or a private university. University costs are going up a lot. Private universities have become very expensive because the government does not help the private schools.

15   Who pays? The parents of children in college may have to pay more, or often the students may have to find jobs. These students have to worry about assignments and grades and also about their jobs. If they work too much at their jobs, they may be absent from class or miss assignments or make

20   too many errors on tests. They may even fail their courses and have to leave the university.

For many students, the problem of getting an education
is not just a problem of homework and exams. They also
have to make money to pay for tuition. And professors don't
25 teach them how to do that!

1. Up to what age is education compulsory in schools in the United

States? _____

_____

2. At what age do most students graduate from high school? _____

_____

3. How many high school graduates go to colleges or universities? _____

_____

4. Do high school students in the United States have to pay tuition?

_____

5. What do college students do if they need money? _____

_____

Follow-up

G. Dictation: Write the sentences that your teacher reads aloud.

1. _____

2. _____

3. _____

4. _____

5. _____

H.   Answer the following questions about your country.

1. Do you have public and private schools?
2. Are private schools very expensive? Public schools?
3. At what age do students finish high school?
4. Do all students go to the same type of high school?
5. Do many young people go on to college or university?
6. Do university students have jobs? What types of jobs?
7. Do they have to pay tuition or other costs?
8. Do parents pay for their children's education at the university level? If not, who pays?
9. Do students always take good notes in classes?

I.   Tell a story about the following situation: John can't pay his tuition and takes a job working at night in a hotel.

Work (A)

Word Form Chart

NOUN	VERB	ADJECTIVE	ADVERB	PREPOSITION OR CONJUNCTION
		annual	annually	
condition				
effort		effortless	effortlessly	
		excellent	excellently	
expectation	expect	expected		
		expectant	expectantly	
	hire	hired		
		hiring		
laziness		lazy	lazily	
		less		
month		monthly	monthly	
owner ⚥	own	owned		
		part-time	part-time	
pride		proud	proudly	
production	produce	productive	productively	
productivity				
salary				
				until

Definitions and Examples

1. **annual** [once a year]

   Most people in the United States have an **annual** vacation of two weeks or more.

   A: Why are you worried?
   B: My **annual** meeting with the boss is tomorrow. We're going to talk about my work during the year.

2. **salary** [the money received for a job each month]

   An employee's **salary** is the same every month. It does not change if he works more hours.

   A: Why are you looking for a new job?
   B: My **salary** is too low. I want to make more money.

3. **condition(s)** [everything around you which may make you feel good or bad]

   "Bad working **conditions**" means an uncomfortable office, unfriendly people, and machines that do not work.
   The working **conditions** in my office are very good. There are many windows, and the furniture is very comfortable.

   A: Why did you leave the classroom?
   B: I can't study under those **conditions**! It's too noisy, and there's no light.

4. **effort** [attempts to work, study, or do things]

   You need a lot of **effort** to finish a big job.
   Ambitious people usually make a big **effort** to succeed.
   That student got an "A" without any **effort**; he never studies!

5. **excellent** [very, very good]

   Employees who do **excellent** work receive good salaries.
   Students who do **excellent** work receive "A's."
   Employees will make a lot of effort for an **excellent** boss.

6. **expect** (to) [to think that something will happen]

   Excellent workers **expect to** get good salaries.

   Employee: When will the boss return from his trip?
   Secretary: His plane will arrive tomorrow at 9:00. I **expect** him to be in the office at 12:00.

7. **hire** [to give a job to; to employ]

    Most companies like to **hire** people with experience.

    A: How was your interview yesterday?
    B: Excellent! I think the company will **hire** me.

8. **lazy** [not liking to work]

    Lazy students do not do their homework and do not study.
    Companies do not like to hire **lazy** people.

9. **less** [not more; not as much as]

    Lazy people do **less** work than ambitious people. They are usually
    less careful than others. Because of this, they get **less** respect
    from their bosses. They might get **less** money, too.

    A: My ticket cost $10.
    B: Oh, mine was **less** expensive. I paid only $8.

10. **monthly** [once a month]

    Most people pay their rent **monthly**.
    In some companies, workers get **monthly** pay. In other places they
    are paid once every two weeks.

11. **own** [to have]

    You **own** something if you bought it or if it was a gift from
    someone.
    Rich people usually **own** many things.

12. **part-time** [fewer hours than a usual job or course]

    Many students work **part-time** to get money for school. They may
    work ten or twenty hours every week.
    University students usually take four or five classes, but **part-time**
    students take only one or two classes.

13. **produce** [to make]

    Factories in Japan **produce** cars and cameras for many countries.
    Italy **produces** shoes.
    An employee who does not make much effort does not **produce**
    much.

14. **pride** [a good feeling because of something that you did well]

    A person who takes **pride** in his work will do a good job.
    A student feels **proud** when he gets an "A."
    I feel **proud** when someone says something nice about my work.

    Boss: I'm **proud** of you. You're doing excellent work!
    Employee: Thank you.

15. until [up to a time]

> Most people in the United States work from 8:30 A.M. **until** 5:00 P.M. every day. They leave the office at 5:00 P.M.
>
> A: How late are you going to stay at the office today?
> B: **Until** the boss leaves. Then I'll go home, too.

Introductory Exercises

A. Match each word with its definition.

   ____ **1.** up to a time   **a.** annually

   ____ **2.** to make   **b.** condition

   ____ **3.** to have   **c.** excellent

   ____ **4.** very, very good   **d.** expect

   ____ **5.** less time than a usual job   **e.** hire

   ____ **6.** one time a month   **f.** lazy

   ____ **7.** one time a year   **g.** monthly

   ____ **8.** to give a job to   **h.** own

   ____ **9.** to think something will be   **i.** part-time

   ____ **10.** a good feeling about work done well   **j.** pride

   ____ **11.** money received for a job   **k.** produce

                                               l. salary

                                               m. until

B. Answer each question with a word from the word form chart in this unit.

1. Should you hire an excellent worker or a lazy one?
2. How do you feel when you do a good job?
3. How often do most people pay rent?
4. How often do most people take a vacation?
5. What type of employee works twenty hours a week?
6. If an excellent worker applies for a job, what should the boss do?
7. What is necessary to complete a lot of work?

Study Exercises

C.   Write **T** if the sentence is true and **F** if it is false.

_____ 1. Ambitious people are usually lazy.

_____ 2. Businesses usually hire people with experience.

_____ 3. Poor people often own two houses.

_____ 4. Most people work part-time.

_____ 5. It takes a lot of effort to move a heavy chair.

_____ 6. People with more experience often receive a higher salary.

_____ 7. If you fail a test, you should be proud.

_____ 8. New Year's Day is an annual holiday in some countries.

_____ 9. Companies like to hire excellent workers.

_____ 10. You can expect that a careful worker will do a good job.

_____ 11. Good working conditions can mean nice employees and a clean office.

D.   Circle the correct word to complete the sentence.

A clerk is looking for a job, and he interviews with your company. He has a lot of experience, and he works very hard at his job now. You decide to hire him. What do you expect?

1. Your company will make $\left\{ \begin{array}{l} \text{more} \\ \text{less} \end{array} \right\}$ with this employee.

2. He will put $\left\{ \begin{array}{l} \text{little} \\ \text{a lot of} \end{array} \right\}$ effort into his work.

3. You $\left\{ \begin{array}{l} \text{will} \\ \text{will not} \end{array} \right\}$ be proud of his work.

4. He $\left\{ \begin{array}{l} \text{will} \\ \text{will not} \end{array} \right\}$ be lazy.

5. The new employee will expect two weeks of vacation $\left\{ \begin{array}{l} \text{monthly} \\ \text{annually} \end{array} \right\}$ from the company.

6. He will want a $\left\{ \begin{array}{l} \text{high} \\ \text{low} \end{array} \right\}$ salary.

7. He will also want $\left\{ \begin{array}{l} \text{excellent} \\ \text{uncomfortable} \end{array} \right\}$ working conditions.

E.   Complete each sentence with a new word.

1. If you do a job well, you feel _____ .

2. Factories in Japan _____ a lot of radios.

3. If a person has a good interview, the company may _____ him.

4. The president _____-s two houses and a boat.

5. His _____ is high, so he does not worry about money.

6. Businesses usually do not hire students _____ they finish school.

7. Bad working _____-s may mean a very cold building and noisy machines.

8. Something that is once a year is _____ .

9. A job that takes only fifteen hours a week is _____ .

10. People who do not like to work are _____ .

11. A magazine that comes every four weeks is a _____ magazine.

12. If you work hard, you can _____ to receive a good salary.

13. Ten is _____ than fifteen.

14. You should try the new restaurant downtown. The food is _____ .

15. It takes a lot of _____ to learn a language.

F.   Read the dialogue and answer the questions that follow.

Kevin Goodwin is applying for a job with a travel company. His interview is at 10:00 with the company's owner, Kathy Anderson. Part of the interview goes like this:

Anderson: Explain your work experiences, Mr. Goodwin.

Goodwin: When I was a student, I worked part-time at the campus travel company. When I graduated, I was hired as a full-time employee. Now I handle travel plans for both professors and students. I also plan the schedules, hotels, and plane trips for guests who visit the university.

Anderson: Why are you interested in our company? Is there a problem with the job you have now?

Goodwin: No, there is no problem. The working conditions are excellent, and working for the university has many advantages. But our business is small, and I would enjoy working for a bigger company like yours.

Anderson: What do you know about our company?

Goodwin: I know that you have the biggest travel company in this city. You have contracts with the city and state governments and also with some big private companies. That's exciting for me. Also, my boss says that, in his opinion, you are the most respected local travel company.

Anderson: Thank you. But it requires a lot of effort to succeed in this business.

Goodwin: Yes. I know some of your employees. I know that you hire only people with excellent skills and that you expect a lot of work from them. They have told me that they rarely work less than 45 hours a week. It's not a job for lazy people, but your employees are proud of the company.

Anderson: Mr. Goodwin, you seem like the type of ambitious young person we need. You already know the salary for this job. Now we need to talk about vacations. Our employees must work one Saturday monthly, but each person may take an annual vacation of three weeks. I won't make a final decision until next week, but you should expect good news at that time.

1. Where is Kevin Goodwin working now? _____

_____

2. When did he begin this job? _____

_____

3. What does Goodwin like about his present job? _____

_____

4. Why does he want to change jobs? _____

_____

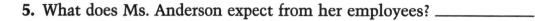

5. What does Ms. Anderson expect from her employees? _____

_____

6. Do Ms. Anderson's employees work part-time? _____

_____

7. How often do the employees work on Saturday? _____

_____

8. How much vacation do the employees get every year? _____

_____

9. Do you think Ms. Anderson will hire Mr. Goodwin? _____

_____

10. In your opinion, why are Ms. Anderson's employees proud of the

company? _____

_____

Follow-up

G. Dictation: Write the sentences that your teacher reads aloud.

1. _____

2. _____

3. _____

4. _____

5. _____

H. Answer the following questions.

1. What kind of weather makes you feel lazy?
2. When do you feel proud?
3. What is your idea of an excellent teacher?
4. Do you think schools should hire more young teachers? Why or why not?

5. In your country, what do students expect from a teacher?
6. Do teachers in your country receive good salaries?
7. What does your country produce?

I. Tell a story about the following situation. What will happen?

Kim is a good worker. She applied for a new job last week, and the boss liked her.

Housing (A)

Word Form Chart

NOUN	VERB	ADJECTIVE	ADVERB
area			
availability		available	
block			
convenience		convenient	conveniently
inconvenience	inconvenience	inconvenient	inconveniently
curtain			
		for sale	
improvement	improve	improved	
location	locate	located	
		nearby	nearby
paint	paint	painted	
pick	pick		
satisfaction	satisfy	satisfied	
		satisfying	
dissatisfaction		dissatisfied	
size			
town			
wood		wood	
		wooden	

Definitions and Examples

1. **area** [a part of a city; a neighborhood; a space]

    The university students all live in the **area** near the campus.

    A: What **area** of the city do you live in?
    B: I live in the **area** near the beach.

2. **convenient** [easy to use; easy to get to]

>   The food store is very **convenient** for me; it is across the street, and it is open until midnight.
>   Our house is in a **convenient** area—near downtown, near the university, and near a bus stop.

3. **available** [open to use, buy, or rent]

>   If a chair is **available** at a movie, you can sit in it.
>   The house that I want to buy will be **available** in June.

>   Student: Do you have any apartments to rent?
>   Landlord: Yes. We have one apartment **available** now and one that will be **available** next month.

4. **block** [the land (usually with buildings) between two streets]

>   I live four **blocks** from the elementary school.
>   The children on my **block** had a swimming party yesterday.
>   Many city **blocks** have both stores and apartment buildings.

5. **location** [the place where something is]

>   The **location** of the school cafeteria is very inconvenient; it is too far from the classrooms.

>   A: What will the **location** of the new airport be?
>   B: The airport will be **located** north of the city.

6. **curtain**

>   Our new house has furniture but no **curtains** at the windows.
>   My kitchen has yellow walls, so I want to buy yellow and white **curtains**.

7. **for sale** [available to be bought]

>   The house next to us is **for sale**; the family is moving.

>   A: Is this car **for sale**?
>   B: No. It's not. Someone bought it yesterday.

8. **paint** [the color that you can put on walls, houses, furniture, etc.]

>   Public mailboxes in the United States are **painted** blue and red.

>   A: What color did you **paint** your house?
>   B: We used white **paint** for the walls and green **paint** for the windows.

9. **improve** [to make something better]

   My landlord needs to **improve** our apartment building; the garage
   door is broken, the heat does not work, and the building needs to
   be painted.

   The city government wants to **improve** the public transportation
   here. They want to have more buses, and they want the buses to
   come more frequently.

10. **nearby** [near, not far from; in the general area]

    We decided to move to the suburbs because there were some good
    schools **nearby**.

    A: Is there a hospital in your area?
    B: Yes. There's one **nearby**, only two blocks from my house.

11. **wood** [part of a tree for making furniture, houses, doors, etc.]

    Many houses in the United States are made of **wood**.
    All the furniture in our house is made of dark **wood** from Thailand.

12. **pick** [to choose]

    We **picked** a brick house because it does not need to be painted.

    A: Why did you **pick** California as your home?
    B: Because it has both mountains and beaches.

13. **satisfied** [happy with something]

    The student was not **satisfied** with his "B" grade; he wanted
    an "A."

    A: Are you **satisfied** with your job?
    B: No. I'm not. It's very boring.

14. **size** [how big something (or someone) is]

    Our house is not a good **size** for our big family. It is too small.

    A: What **size** shirt do you wear?
    B: I usually wear a "Large."

15. **town** [a city, usually a small city]

    My **town** is proud of its beautiful park.

    A: What **town** are you from in France?
    B: I'm from a small **town** outside of Paris.

Introductory Exercises

A. Match each word with its definition.

_____ 1. to choose
_____ 2. not far from
_____ 3. to make something better
_____ 4. the land between two streets
_____ 5. a small city
_____ 6. easy to use
_____ 7. material from a tree
_____ 8. place where something is
_____ 9. open to rent

a. area
b. available
c. block
d. convenient
e. curtain
f. improve
g. location
h. nearby
i. paint
j. pick
k. satisfied
l. town
m. wood

B. Answer each question with a word from the word form chart in this unit.

1. What do you put in front of a window?
2. What can you build a barn with?
3. What feeling do you have when you get a good grade in a class?
4. What can you do to an old house?
5. If you want to sell your car, what words can you write on it?
6. You live on First Street. Your friend lives on Third Street. How far from you does your friend live?
7. What is a small city?

Study Exercises

C. In the blanks, write the appropriate word(s) from the word form chart in this unit. Use each word only once.

1. The advantage of this apartment is its _____ close to the university.
2. There are three churches on the _____ between First Street and Second Street.
3. Are you _____ with the _____ of your apartment?
4. Students in the United States can _____ their classes in the university. They may choose their courses.

5. What _____ of the city is the post office in?

6. The landlord _____-d the house by buying new furniture.

7. Information about the new tuition will not be _____ until next week. We will not have the information until then.

8. Is it _____ for you to live so far from your office?

D. Circle the word which is different.

1. location   block   satisfaction
2. paint   improve   available
3. nearby   convenient   for sale
4. pick   town   area

E. Rewrite the following to make correct sentences.

1. inconvenient / is / the schedule / the language lab / of

_____

2. gloves / my / are not / these / size

_____

3. are often painted / barns / red / wooden / in the United States

_____

4. red curtains / picked / her room / the child / for

_____

5. my improvement / satisfy / the teacher / did not

_____

6. this town / available / information / at the library / on / is

_____

F. Read the passage and do the true/false exercise that follows.

      I am the owner of a small clothing store. Three months
ago I decided to move my store to Glendale, another area of
town, because business was not very good. Now I rent store
space in an old building. The new location in Glendale is
5 excellent, and my sales have improved a lot. (The utilities are

also cheaper!) There is a high school nearby, and many of the students come to my store to buy their clothes. This location has other advantages, too. It is closer to my home, and there is a food store on the next block, so it is convenient for me
10 to go shopping after work.

The size of my new store is better too. It is much bigger, and there is a lot of storage space. But the building was not in very good condition, and I had to make many improvements. The paint was old and dirty, and I had to pick a new
15 color and paint all of the walls. I hired a man to build new wooden dressing rooms. I also made new curtains for the rooms and the window. I am completely satisfied with the store now. Unfortunately, I learned last week that the owner wants to sell the building—after all my hard work! How did
20 I learn this? I came to work Friday and saw a "For Sale" sign in front of my store!

_____ 1. The store owner wanted to move to the new location because there was a food store nearby.

_____ 2. She sells clothes to high school students in the area.

_____ 3. It is convenient for the store owner to go shopping because the clothes store is close to her house.

_____ 4. The old store was smaller than the new store.

_____ 5. The landlord of the building made a lot of improvements to the building.

_____ 6. The store owner painted the new store.

_____ 7. She is very satisfied with the new store.

_____ 8. She wants to sell the store.

Follow-up

G. Dictation: Write the sentences that your teacher reads aloud.

1. _____

2. _____

3. _____

4. _____

5. _____

H.   Answer the following questions.

1. What area of town do you live in?
2. What is the most convenient time for you to receive telephone calls?
3. What size is your hometown?
4. What gives you the most satisfaction at school?
5. Why did you pick this school to study at?
6. How can you improve your English?
7. What color is your bedroom painted?
8. How many blocks do you live from the closest bus stop?

I.   Describe the picture.

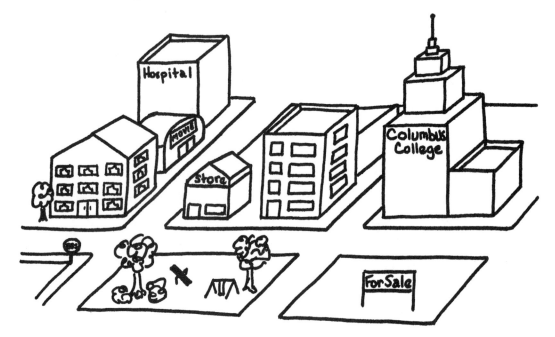

Food

Word Form Chart

NOUN	VERB	ADJECTIVE	ADVERB
bag			
baker ⚲	bake	baked	
bakery		baking	
boil	boil	boiled	
		boiling	
cake			
hunger	hunger	hungry	hungrily
lid			
oven			
pot			
potato			
preference	prefer	preferable	preferably
preparation	prepare	prepared	
refrigerator	refrigerate	refrigerated	
stove			
sweetness	sweeten	sweet	
		sweetened	

Definitions and Examples

1. **sweet** [with a lot of sugar]

    Put a lot of sugar in my coffee. I like it **sweet**.
    Some fruits are **sweet**.

2. **potato** [a vegetable that grows in the ground]

    People in the United States like to eat **potatoes**.

    A: Do people in your country eat a lot of **potatoes**?
    B: No. They like rice better.

3. **bag** [a thing, often made of paper, for carrying items]

    I bought four **bags** of food at the store today.

    A: I bought two five-pound **bags** of potatoes. Will
       you carry one **bag**?
    B: O.K. I'll carry one.

4. **pot** [something used to cook food in]

    Joan cooked the rice in a **pot**.

    A: What type of **pot** should I use to cook the soup?
    B: Use a big one.

5. **stove** [a machine which heats food for cooking]

    You cook soup in a pot on the **stove**.

    A: What foods can you cook on a **stove**?
    B: Rice, eggs, and many other foods.

6. **boil** [when water, milk, etc. turn to gas because they are very hot]

    You must **boil** water on the stove to make tea or coffee.

    A: At what temperature does water **boil**?
    B: At 212° F or 100° C.

7. **lid** [the part that you put on the top of a pot to close it]

    A **lid** makes the heat stay in a pot.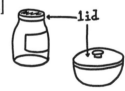

    A: When should I put the **lid** on the pot?
    B: Put it on when the water begins to boil.

8. **oven** [the inside part of a stove where food is heated]

    Bread is made in an **oven**.

    A: What foods can you make in an **oven**?
    B: Bread, fish, potatoes, and lot of other things.

9. **bake** [to cook in an oven]

    My mother **bakes** bread every week.

    A: Does your grandmother **bake** bread?
    B: Yes. She **bakes** every Monday.

10. **cake** [a sweet baked food]

>   My mother bakes a **cake** every Sunday.
>
>   A: How do you bake a **cake**?
>   B: You bake it in the oven.

11. **prepare** (a) [to make]

>   My mother **prepares** breakfast, lunch, and dinner every day.
>
>   A: Who **prepared** your dinner last night?
>   B: My friend did.

>   (b) [to get ready]

>   To **prepare** for a test, you should study.

12. **prefer** [to like one thing better than another]

>   I do not like to eat in restaurants. I **prefer** to prepare my dinner at home.
>
>   A: Would you like coffee or tea?
>   B: I **prefer** tea.

13. **refrigerator** [a machine to make food cold]

>   You should always put milk in the **refrigerator**.
>
>   A: Is it necessary to **refrigerate** meat?
>   B: Yes, it is.
>   A: Should you put fruit in the **refrigerator** too?
>   B: Not always.

14. **hunger** [the need for food]

>   **Hunger** is a big problem in the world today. Many people do not have enough food to eat.
>
>   A: Why is that baby crying?
>   B: I think he's **hungry**. It's time for his dinner.

Introductory Exercises

A. Match each word with its definition.

_____ 1. the part of a stove used for baking
_____ 2. to cook in an oven
_____ 3. a vegetable
_____ 4. to get ready for cooking
_____ 5. the need for food
_____ 6. with a lot of sugar
_____ 7. to like one thing better than another
_____ 8. a machine to make food cold
_____ 9. a sweet baked food

a. bake
b. cake
c. hunger
d. lid
e. oven
f. pot
g. potato
h. prefer
i. prepare
j. refrigerator
k. sweet

B. Answer each question with a word from the word chart in this unit.

1. What is something you put on a pot?
2. Where do you put food to make it cold?
3. What part of a stove is used for baking?
4. What is the name of a sweet baked food?
5. What happens to water at 212° F/100° C?
6. What are people who need food?
7. What can you put food in to cook it?
8. What vegetable do Americans like to eat?
9. Which word means to make food?
10. What is made of paper and used for carrying things?

Study Exercises

C. Write **T** if the sentence is true and **F** if it is false.

_____ 1. You can make food cold on a stove.
_____ 2. People use bags for carrying things.
_____ 3. You bake a cake in an oven.
_____ 4. When people do not need food, they are hungry.
_____ 5. If you like rice better than potatoes, you prefer rice.
_____ 6. A potato that is cooked in an oven is boiled.
_____ 7. You can use a bag to bring food from the store.

____ **8.** People bake bread in an oven.

____ **9.** You should not refrigerate milk.

____ **10.** You cook soup in a pot on the stove.

D. In the blanks, write the appropriate word(s) from the word form chart in this unit.

1. _____ people need food.

2. Cakes are _____ because we prepare them with a lot of sugar.

3. Foods like milk and meat should be put in a _____ .

4. My mother _____-d my dinner last night.

5. Mrs. Jones used to _____ bread every week.

6. You cook soup and rice on a _____ .

7. Her mother and father _____ Italian food, but she likes Chinese food better.

8. When you put a _____ on a pot, the water _____-s sooner.

9. Mary bought ten pounds of _____-es yesterday.

E. Read the passage and answer the questions that follow.

   One day John and Mary decided to prepare dinner
because their mother was sick. At first, they did not know
what food to make. Mary wanted to prepare chicken and rice,
and John wanted to prepare meat and potatoes. When they
5   asked their father to decide, he said the he preferred meat
and potatoes.
   They did not have any potatoes, so John went to the
store and bought a five-pound bag. While John was gone,
Mary took the meat out of the refrigerator, put salt on it, and
10 put it in the oven to bake. When John returned, he put the
potatoes in a pot to boil. Mary put a lid on the pot so the
potatoes would cook faster. Then they decided to make
a cake.
   When dinner was ready, John helped Mary carry the food
15 from the stove to the table. Everyone was very hungry and
liked the food.

1. Why did John and Mary decide to make dinner? _____

_____

2. Who preferred meat and potatoes? _____

_____

3. How did John prepare the potatoes? _____

_____

4. Why did John go to the store? _____

_____

5. What did Mary do while John went to the store? _____

_____

6. Who put the lid on the pot? _____

_____

7. What other food did John and Mary prepare? _____

_____

8. Who was hungry? _____

_____

Follow-up

F. Dictation: Write the sentences that your teacher reads aloud.

1. _____

2. _____

3. _____

4. _____

5. _____

G. Answer the following questions about your country.

1. At what time do people eat dinner?
2. What food(s) do people prefer to eat for breakfast?
3. Who prepares dinner?
4. Are most foods boiled or baked?
5. Do all families have stoves and refrigerators?
6. Do people usually bake bread and cakes or do they buy them?
7. Do stores give people paper bags to carry their food in?
8. How often do people buy food? (every day? once a week?)
9. Do men cook or bake?
10. What do you think is the best food of your country?

H. Tell how you prepare a certain food or drink. (Examples: rice, tea, a cake)

Family

Word Form Chart

NOUN	VERB	ADJECTIVE	ADVERB	PREPOSITION
		alone	alone	
				among
anniversary				
couple ⚥				
divorce	divorce	divorced		
		identical	identically	
joy		joyful	joyfully	
member ⚥				
niece ⚥				
nephew ⚥				
pregnancy		pregnant		
relative ⚥		related		
relation ⚥				
		single		
twin(s) ⚥		twin		
wedding				

Definitions and Examples

1. **alone** [with no one else]

    Her grandmother lived **alone** in that big house.

    A: I thought you were going to see a movie.
    B: Why don't you come with me? I don't want to go **alone**.

2. **divorce** [the end of a marriage]

    After they were married for almost 25 years, they got a **divorce**.

    A: Where's your husband?
    B: Haven't you heard? We were **divorced** last month.

3. **anniversary** [the date of the passing of another year after the time of something important]

    Her aunt and uncle have been married for many years. They had their twentieth **anniversary** this year.

    A: How long have you been married?
    B: We're having our seventh **anniversary** next month.

4. **couple** [a man and a woman]

    A young **couple** moved into the house across the street.

    A: Who lives in that apartment?
    B: A married **couple** with two children.

5. **related** [of the same family]

    They look the same, but they're not **related**.

    A: Do you know him?
    B: Yes. We're **relatives**. My aunt married his brother.

6. **joy** [happiness]

    There was not much **joy** in the house when my grandmother was sick.

    A: Let's not have a party this year.
    B: But why not? An anniversary should be a time of **joy**.

7. **member** [a person in a family or a group]

    All the **members** of the family came to the grandparents' anniversary party.

    A: Why didn't you go to the party?
    B: I don't know them very well. It was for family **members**.

8. **pregnant** [going to have a baby]

    His brother's wife is **pregnant** again, for the fifth time.

    A: My wife is **pregnant**.
    B: Congratulations! When do you expect the baby?
    A: In March.

9. **single** [not married]

   Single people usually have more free time than married couples.

   A: Are you married or **single**?
   B: **Single**.

10. **twins** [two children born at the same time of the same mother]

    My sister has **twins**. She always dresses them both the same.

    A: Congratulations! A boy or a girl?
    B: Two boys. **Twins**.

11. **wedding** [when two people get married]

    My brother's **wedding** is next Saturday. All the family members
       will be there.

    A: Where's the **wedding**?
    B: At a church downtown.

12. **identical** [the same, having no differences]

    Those **identical** twins look the same.
    The teacher was not happy because their test papers were **identical**;
       they made the same mistakes.

13. **niece** [the daughter of your brother or sister]

    My **niece** is ten years old.

    A: How many **nieces** do you have?
    B: Two.

14. **nephew** [the son of your brother or sister]

    Ali has three **nephews** and no nieces.
    My **nephew** is a music student.

15. **among** [of (a group)]

    I am the youngest **among** my brothers and sisters.
    Among the American presidents, Kennedy was well liked around
       the world.

Introductory Exercises

A. Match each word with its definition.

    ____ **1.** two children born at the same time of the same mother

    ____ **2.** the son of your brother or sister

    ____ **3.** the end of a marriage

    ____ **4.** not married

    ____ **5.** going to have a baby

    ____ **6.** having no differences

    ____ **7.** happiness

    ____ **8.** a man and a woman

    ____ **9.** the daughter of your brother or sister

a. alone
b. among
c. anniversary
d. couple
e. divorce
f. identical
g. joy
h. member
i. nephew
j. niece
k. pregnant
l. related
m. single
n. twins
o. wedding

B. Complete the sentence with a word from the word form chart.

    1. My grandmother lived in the big house _____ .

    2. His brother married my aunt, so we are _____ .

    3. A wedding is a time for _____ .

    4. The anniversary party was only for family _____ -s .

    5. The marriage ended in _____ .

    6. They have four children, and she's _____ again.

    7. My father married young, but his brother has always remained

    _____ .

    8. Those twins look the same. They are _____ twins.

    9. _____ my relatives, he is the oldest.

    10. They were prepared for one child but not for _____ .

    11. Fred, my _____ , is my sister Nancy's son.

Study Exercises

C. Write **T** if the sentence is true and **F** if it is false.

_____ 1. Wedding anniversaries come once every three years.

_____ 2. A divorce is usually a time of great joy.

_____ 3. Family members are all related to each other.

_____ 4. All people have nephews and nieces.

_____ 5. Most children are not twins.

_____ 6. His wife is single.

_____ 7. Many people get married for the first time when they are old.

_____ 8. Identical things are very different.

_____ 9. Your niece is usually younger than you are.

D. Write sentences with the words.

1. next / the wedding / be / December / will

   _____

2. the same / twins / look / may

   _____

3. across / the young couple / a divorce / the street / got

   _____

4. a time/ was / joy /great / the anniversary / of

   _____

5. of the family / after / came / the wedding / friends / to the party / and members (more than one correct answer)

   _____

6. the fourth time / she's / for / pregnant

   _____

7. divorced / of my relatives / are / many

   _____

8. ambitious / is / my / very / nephew

E.   **I.** Match each word with a word or phrase that has the same meaning.

      ____ **1.** wedding   **a.** same

      ____ **2.** joy   **b.** age

                                c. not married

      ____ **3.** single   **d.** working hard

      ____ **4.** identical   **e.** pregnant

                                f. brother's daughter

      ____ **5.** niece   **g.** marriage

                                h. happiness

                                i. father's sister

II. Match each word with the word or phrase that has the opposite meaning.

      ____ **1.** single   **a.** divorce

      ____ **2.** wedding   **b.** family members

                                  c. sadness

      ____ **3.** joy   **d.** anniversary

      ____ **4.** identical   **e.** married

                                  f. lazy

                                g. different

F.   Read the passage and answer the questions that follow.

Most of the members of my family married young. Many of them were also divorced young, before the age of 30. Few of them had much joy in their married life, but they continued to look for it, again and again. Only my Aunt
5 Margaret was different.

She lived alone until she was nearly 35. But she always loved weddings. She went to all the weddings of her brothers and sisters and cousins and friends. She saw many of these people have painful divorces, but if they decided to marry
10 again, Aunt Margaret was always at their second weddings.

We thought that she would remain a single woman. She was very busy and seemed to be happy to spend time with her brothers and sisters and their children. Nobody thought that the woman who had seen over a hundred weddings
15 would marry. But she did.

To our surprise she met a man—at a wedding—and married him two months later. She did not tell many people about her plans, and few relatives were asked to come to her wedding. It was small and private.
20 We were even more surprised later to learn that she was pregnant. At the age of 36 she had a baby boy. Most of her

brothers and sisters had children in high school by that time. Two years later she was pregnant again, and this time she had twin boys.

25 Unlike her brothers and sisters she stayed married to the same person. She was the same Aunt Margaret, but she did not have much time for her relatives anymore. And there was one other change in her life. She did not like to go to weddings anymore.

30 "Never again," she said. "Not until my boys get married."

1. At what age did the members of this family usually get married? ___

_____

2. Did the marriages last? _____

_____

3. How was Aunt Margaret different? _____

_____

4. What did she like to do? _____

_____

5. Why was her family surprised when she married? _____

_____

6. Where did she meet her husband? _____

_____

7. How did she change? _____

_____

8. Will she ever go to a wedding again? _____

_____

Follow-up

G. Dictation: Write the sentences that your teacher reads aloud.

1. _____

2. _____

3. _____

4. _____

5. _____

H. Answer the following questions about your country.

1. At what age do people get married?
2. Do very many marriages end in divorce?
3. Is it difficult to get a divorce?
4. Do many people wait until they are over 30 before they marry?
5. Do women over 35 have children?
6. Are weddings large or small?
7. Do people have a party after a wedding?
8. What do people do on their wedding anniversary?
9. How do uncles and aunts feel about their nephews and nieces?

I. Tell a story about the following situation. What will happen?

John remained single until he was nearly 35 years old.

Health

Word Form Chart

NOUN	VERB	ADJECTIVE	ADVERB
blanket	blanket		
blindness	blind	blind	blindly
breath	breathe	breathless	breathlessly
condition			
cure	cure	cured	
dentist ⚥		dental	
death	die	dead	
		deadly	
disease		diseased	
exercise	exercise		
fee			
injury	injure	injured	
		injurious	
patient ⚥			
rest	rest	rested	
		resting	
tooth (teeth)			
x-ray	x-ray		

Definitions and Examples

1. **die** [to stop living]

   The sick man **died** last night.
   President Kennedy **died** in 1963.

2. **tooth** {plural: **teeth**} [the hard, white parts in your mouth used for eating]

    Small babies do not have any **teeth**.
    My **tooth** hurt very much, so I could not eat.

3. **blind** [not able to see]

    If you are **blind**, you cannot see.
    The **blind** man's dog helped him walk down the street.

4. **breathe** [to take air in and out by your nose or mouth]

    People must **breathe** to live.
    People cannot **breathe** in water.
    The woman had difficulty **breathing** because she was sick.

5. **disease** [a sickness]

    His **disease** was very bad, and he died.
    Her **disease** made breathing a problem.

6. **cure** [to make a disease better]

    The medicine **cured** the disease in one week.
    Some diseases cannot be **cured**.

    A: What's the **cure** for your problem?
    B: The doctor gave me some medicine.

7. **dentist** [a doctor for teeth]

    I went to the **dentist** because my tooth hurt.
    Many people do not like to visit their **dentists**.

8. **fee** [the money you must pay for work done by a doctor or dentist]

    I stopped going to that doctor because his **fees** were very high.

    A: How much is that dentist's **fee** for an examination?
    B: Forty dollars.

9. **exercise** [to make your body work]

    Many people **exercise** every day to stay healthy.
    Running is excellent **exercise**.

10. **patient** [a sick person who is in the hospital, or who is seeing a doctor or dentist]

    There are more than 200 **patients** in that hospital.
    Some **patients** were waiting to see the doctor.

11. **injury** [the hurt to a body]

    His **injuries** were very bad, and he died.
    Many people were **injured** in the fighting.

12. **blanket** [the thing on your bed to make you warm]

> The patient was cold, so the nurse put a **blanket** on him.
> It was so cold yesterday that I slept with three **blankets**.

13. **rest** [to not work or not move]

> The doctor told me to **rest** in bed for two days.
>
> A: Are you sleeping?
> B: No. I'm only **resting**.

14. **condition** [how a person or thing is]

> His **condition** is very bad because of his injuries.
> My car is in bad **condition**. It does not start.
>
> A: What is the **condition** of the patient?
> B: She's fine.

15. **x-ray** [a picture of the inside of a body]

> The **x-ray** showed that his leg was broken.
> Dentists often take **x-rays** of people's teeth.

Introductory Exercises

A. Match each word with its definition.

____ **1.** to make your body work	**a.** blanket
____ **2.** a doctor for teeth	**b.** blind
____ **3.** how a person or thing is	**c.** breathe
____ **4.** a picture of the inside of a body	**d.** condition
____ **5.** to take in air	**e.** cure
____ **6.** a hard, white thing in your mouth	**f.** dentist
____ **7.** to make a disease better	**g.** die
____ **8.** to not work or not move	**h.** disease
____ **9.** a sickness	**i.** exercise
____ **10.** not able to see	**j.** fee
____ **11.** the money you must pay a doctor or dentist	**k.** injury
____ **12.** a sick person	**l.** patient
____ **13.** hurt to a body	**m.** rest
	n. tooth
	o. x-ray

B. Answer with a word from the word form chart in this unit.

    1. What must you pay a doctor?
    2. What do people do with air?
    3. Whom do you find in hospitals?
    4. What do you use to sleep under when it is cold?
    5. Whom do you visit when your tooth hurts?
    6. What do you do when you stop living?
    7. What do most people do at night?
    8. What does medicine do?
    9. What is running?
  10. What is another word for **sickness**?

Study Exercises

C. Write **T** if the sentence is true and **F** if it is false.

    _____ 1. Patients like high fees.
    _____ 2. Running is resting.
    _____ 3. Blind people cannot see.
    _____ 4. Medicine can cure some diseases.
    _____ 5. People can breathe in water.
    _____ 6. Patients who are in good condition often die.
    _____ 7. You can see the inside of teeth on an x-ray.
    _____ 8. Dentists help blind people to see.
    _____ 9. People can die from diseases and injuries.
  _____ 10. We use blankets when the weather is hot.

D. Circle the word which is different.

    1. dentist   patient   doctor
    2. rest   blindness   injury
    3. tuition   rest   fee
    4. tooth   nose   blanket
    5. hurt   cure   injure
    6. fee   payment   medicine

E. In the blank, write the appropriate word(s) from the word form chart in this unit.

1. He went to the _____ because he has a problem with his teeth.

2. The doctor thought my arm was broken, so he decided to take an _____ .

3. The patient is in very good _____ ; he can leave the hospital tomorrow.

4. A broken leg is an _____ .

5. If you are too fat, you should _____ .

6. If a person cannot breathe, he will _____ .

7. If the night is cold, you should use a _____ when you sleep.

8. If you cannot see, you are _____ .

9. Your _____ are in your mouth.

10. The sick people in a hospital are _____ -s .

11. When you go to a dentist, you usually pay a _____ .

12. The doctor gave her medicine but did not _____ her disease.

Follow-up

F. Dictation: Write the sentences that your teacher reads aloud.

1. _____

2. _____

3. _____

4. _____

5. _____

G. Answer the following questions.

1. Have you ever had an x-ray? Why?
2. How often do you go to a dentist?
3. Do you pay a fee to see a dentist in your country? How much is the fee?

4. How do you exercise? How often?
5. In your country, during which months do people need blankets to sleep?
6. Do you pay a fee to see a doctor in your country? How much is the fee?
7. What types of exercise are common in your country?
8. Have you had any injuries this year? What type?
9. Where do doctors see their patients in your country?

H. Complete the stories.

1. John's tooth hurts . . .
2. Mary is having problems breathing . . .

UNIT
7

Crime

Word Form Chart

NOUN	VERB	ADJECTIVE	ADVERB
attack	attack	attacking	
attacker ⚥			
arrest	arrest	arrested	
		arresting	
avoidance	avoid	avoidable	avoidably
beating	beat (beat, beaten)	beaten	
court			
courtroom			
gang ⚥			
investigation	investigate	investigative	
		investigated	
		investigating	
judge ⚥	judge	judgmental	judgmentally
judgment			
lie	lie	lying	
lock	lock	locked	
	unlock	unlocked	
robbery	rob	robbed	
robber ⚥			
scare	scare	scary	
		scared	
silence	silence	silent	silently
value	value	valuable	
victim ⚥	victimize	victimized	

48

Definitions and Examples

1. **silent** [with no noise]

    > The street was **silent** at midnight.
    > The teacher wanted **silence** during the test.

2. **lie** (about) [to not tell the truth]

    > The little boy **lied** to his mother about the broken window; he said
    >   that his sister had broken it, but he had.
    > The murderer **lied about** where he had been at the time of the
    >   murder.
    > You cannot trust a person who **lies**.

3. **rob** [to take something from someone; to steal]

    > He **robbed** a bank and stole ten thousand dollars.

    > A: How much money did the **robber** take from you?
    > B: Only twenty dollars.

4. **lock** [to shut a door or window with a key]

    > If you do not **lock** your door, someone may rob you.

    > A: Did he **lock** the door?
    > B: Yes. I saw the key in his hand.

5. **attack** [to try to hurt someone or something]

    > They **attacked** their enemies and fought for three hours.
    > The old man was **attacked** and killed at midnight.

6. **gang** [a group, often of criminals or of young men, who make trouble]

    > Everyone is frightened of that **gang** because they commit many
    >   crimes.
    > He was attacked by a **gang**, who also robbed him.

7. **beat** (a) [to hit someone many times]

    > A gang robbed and **beat** the old woman.
    > Some bigger boys gave the little boy a **beating**.

    (b) [to make someone lose, for example, a game; to win]

    > Our baseball team **beat** the one from the next town.

8. **victim** [a person who has a bad experience; the person who is hurt by a
    crime]

    > The man was the **victim** of an attack.
    > The murder **victim** was found in her house.
    > Many **victims** of the war lost their families.

9. **scare** [to frighten]

    The attack on the old woman **scared** many of the older people in the town.
    A horror movie may **scare** the children.
    Many people are **scared** to walk alone at night.

10. **valuable** [expensive or important; something that you do not want to lose]

    There are some very **valuable** things in that house; they should lock the door carefully.
    A: What's the **value** of that car?
    B: Fifteen thousand dollars.

11. **arrest** [to find someone and hold him, usually done by the police]

    The police **arrested** the robbers soon after the robbery.
    The men who were **arrested** were taken to jail.

12. **judge** (a) [a government person who decides if someone has broken the law or not]

    The **judge** sent the murderer to jail for many years.
    Judges are often very respected people.

    (b) [to give an opinion about the value of something; to say if something is good or bad]

    The president's advisers **judged** the trip to be too dangerous for him.
    In my **judgment**, you made the wrong decision.

13. **court** [the government place where judges work]

    The criminal was taken to the **court**, and the judge decided how long he should stay in jail.
    Lawyers and judges work in **courtrooms**.

14. **investigate** [to try to find the truth about a mystery or a crime; to examine]

    The police **investigate** crimes.
    The **investigation** of the murder lasted for a month.

15. **avoid** [to try not to go somewhere or not to do something]

    You should **avoid** walking alone at night.
    If a person wants to lose weight, he should **avoid** sweet foods.

Introductory Exercises

A. Match each word with its definition.

_____ 1. to shut a door with a key
_____ 2. to not tell the truth
_____ 3. expensive
_____ 4. to hit someone many times
_____ 5. a group of criminals
_____ 6. to try to hurt someone
_____ 7. a person who has a bad experience
_____ 8. to frighten
_____ 9. to take something from someone
_____ 10. with no noise
_____ 11. to try not to do something
_____ 12. to decide if a person has broken the law
_____ 13. to try to find the truth about a crime
_____ 14. the government place where judges work

a. arrest
b. attack
c. avoid
d. beat
e. court
f. gang
g. investigate
h. judge
i. lie
j. lock
k. rob
l. scare
m. silent
n. valuable
o. victim

B. Answer each question with a word from the word form chart in this unit.

1. What do criminals do to banks?
2. What should you do about dangerous places?
3. What do the police do to criminals?
4. What is something if you paid a lot for it?
5. What do you do if you don't tell the truth?
6. Who works in a court?
7. What do the police do about crimes?
8. What do you do to a door with a key?
9. What does an army do to an enemy army?
10. What is a group of criminals?

Study Exercises

C. Write **T** if the sentence is true and **F** if it is false.

_____ **1.** Sometimes robbers can open locked doors.

_____ **2.** Victims of crimes are often scared later.

_____ **3.** People do not want to avoid attacks.

_____ **4.** The police arrest criminals.

_____ **5.** If you are attacked, you should be silent.

_____ **6.** Robbers want to steal valuable things.

_____ **7.** Criminals never lie.

_____ **8.** Attackers investigate crimes.

_____ **9.** Many people are scared of gangs.

_____**10.** Judges avoid courtrooms.

D. In the blanks, write the appropriate word(s) from the word form chart in this unit.

1. She carefully _____-ed the door when she left the house.

2. The gang of criminals _____-ed the man and left him lying in the street.

3. The police are _____-ing the _____ of the bank.

4. The _____ decided to send the _____ to prison for fifteen years because he stole so much money.

5. The _____ of the beating was badly hurt.

6. The judge did not trust the murderer because he knew he

   _____-d .

7. During the _____ , the police found the gun which the murderer used.

E. Read the passage and answer the questions that follow.

Last night our neighbors' house was robbed. A gang of four robbers climbed the fence around their house and then broke the lock on their back door to get into the house. They worked so silently that we did not hear anything. The
5   robbers had chosen a time when no one was in the house, so

no one was hurt. But the family was scared when they saw that many of their valuable things were gone.

The police who came to investigate the robbery told the family that they were the third victims of robbery in the
10 neighborhood that week. The police told them to avoid leaving the house dark at night and to be careful to lock all the doors and windows.

Later that night, the police arrested four men who had some of the stolen things from our neighbors' house. The
15 men said that they had not committed the robbery, but the police think that they are lying. The men will have to go to court.

1. How did the robbers get into the house? _____

_____

2. Why didn't we hear any noise? _____

_____

3. What was taken from the house? _____

_____

4. How many families had been robbed that week? _____

5. What should they do to avoid future robberies? _____

_____

6. What did the police do when they found the men with the stolen

things? _____

_____

Follow-up

F. Dictation: Write the sentences that your teacher reads aloud.

1. _____

2. _____

3. _____

4. _____

5. _____

G. Answer the following questions.

1. Do people in your country lock their doors? When?
2. Where can you find silence?
3. Have you been the victim of a crime or do you know anyone who was a victim? Explain.
4. Who decides how long a criminal stays in jail in your country?
5. Are people scared to walk alone at night in your city? Why?
6. What types of things do people lie about? Why?
7. What types of places do you avoid going to? Why?
8. Do the police arrest most robbers in your country?
9. How many judges are there in a court in your country?
10. Do the police have trouble with gangs of young men in your country? What kinds of things do the gangs do?

H. Describe a crime which you have heard of or experienced.

Military

Word Form Chart

NOUN	VERB	ADJECTIVE	ADVERB	PREPOSITION
				above
bomb	bomb	bombed		
command	command	commanding	commandingly	
commander 人				
control	control	controlled		
controller 人		controlling		
damage	damage	damaged		
		damaging		
defeat	defeat	defeated		
defense	defend	defensive	defensively	
		defending		
destruction	destroy	destroyed		
		destructive	destructively	
guy 人				
march	march	marching		
officer 人				
rank		ranking		
sailor 人	sail	sailing		
	sink (sank, sunk)	sinking		
		sunken		
surrender	surrender	surrendering		

Definitions and Examples

1. **above** [over]

   The plane flew high **above** the city.
   There is a light in the room **above** our heads.

2. **guy** (informal) [a person, usually a man]

   Many young **guys** become soldiers.

   A: Do you like John?
   B: Yes. He's a nice **guy**.

3. **damage** [to hurt things]

   Many buildings were **damaged** during the war.
   I **damaged** my television when I moved it.

4. **defeat** [to make someone else lose; to beat]

   Our army **defeated** theirs.
   They tried to **defeat** their enemies.

5. **defend** [to take care of yourself when you are attacked]

   They **defended** their city against the attack of the enemy.
   The military **defends** the country.

6. **destroy** [to damage something completely]

   We will have to build that house again; it is **destroyed**.

   A: What **destroyed** this area of the city?
   B: An attack by the enemy during the last war.

   During the war, the **destruction** of the city was complete.

7. **sail** [to move on top of water, as a ship moves]

   That ship **sails** across the ocean.
   I like to go **sailing** on the lake.
   My brother is a **sailor** in the navy.

8. **sink** [to go down under the water]

   Many sailors were killed when their ship **sank**.
   My keys **sank** in the water and disappeared.
   The people swam away from their **sinking** ship.

9. **surrender** [to stop fighting because you are losing]

   Germany **surrendered** at the end of World War II.
   The soldiers could not defend the area, so they **surrendered**.

10. **bomb** [a thing often used in wars which can kill many people and destroy buildings]

    Much of the town was destroyed by **bombs**.
    The **bomb** in the car killed four people.

11. **officer** [an important person in the military]

    The **officers** in the army make the decisions.
    The **officer** told the soldiers to continue working.

12. **rank** [how important a person is in a group, often the military]

    An officer has high **rank**.
    Most soldiers have low **rank**.

13. **control** [to take care of; to make someone do something]

    Parents should **control** their children.
    Officers in the military **control** the soldiers of lower rank.

14. **command** [to control; to tell people of lower rank to do something]

    The officer **commanded** his men to guard the town.
    The soldiers must do what they are **commanded** to do.

    A: Who is in **command** here?
    B: That officer is.

15. **march** [to walk with many other people; to walk in a parade]

    The soldiers **marched** in the parade.
    They **marched** for so long that their feet hurt.

Introductory Exercises

A. Match each word with its definition.

____	**1.** an important person in the military	**a.**	above
____	**2.** over	**b.**	bomb
____	**3.** to take care of yourself when you are attacked	**c.**	command
____	**4.** an informal word that means person	**d.**	control
____	**5.** to stop fighting in defeat	**e.**	damage
____	**6.** a person who works on a boat	**f.**	defeat
____	**7.** to walk in a parade	**g.**	defend
____	**8.** to go down under water	**h.**	destroy
____	**9.** how important a person is in the military	**i.**	guy
____	**10.** a thing which destroys buildings and kills people	**j.**	march
____	**11.** to win	**k.**	officer
____	**12.** to hurt things	**l.**	rank
____	**13.** to damage all of something	**m.**	sailor
		n.	sink
		o.	surrender

B. Answer **TRUE** or **FALSE**.

1. Bombs can destroy buildings.
2. An officer has low rank.
3. When you defeat someone, you win.
4. Soldiers sometimes march.
5. An army which is winning will surrender.
6. Only women are guys.
7. You look up to see something above you.
8. The navy has a lot of sailors.
9. Bombs sometimes sink ships.

Study Exercises

C. Circle the word which is different.

1. defend   destroy   damage
2. sailor   rank   officer
3. surrender   control   command
4. sail   march   guy
5. bomb   gun   rank
6. above   officer   soldier

D. In the blanks, write the appropriate word(s) from the word form chart in this unit.

1. When the _____ damaged the ship, the ship
   _____ and the sailors were killed.
2. The soldiers _____-ed in the military parade.
3. An officer has a high _____ in the military.
4. Because they knew that they were going to lose, the soldiers
   _____-ed .
5. Many young _____-s enter the navy and become sailors.
6. The plans flew _____ the city.
7. The officer was in _____ of 100 soldiers.
8. The bombs from the planes _____-ed many buildings.
9. If someone attacks you, you need to _____ yourself.

E. Read the passage and answer the questions that follow.

> The attack was early in the morning. The bombs from the enemy planes destroyed half of the city. Many buildings which were not destroyed were damaged. Our air force tried to defend the city, but soon many of our planes were
> 5 destroyed. Many of our ships sailing in the waters near the coast were sunk by the bombs. Finally, our army officers commanded their men to march out of the city, which they could not defend. By late afternoon, the city had surrendered.

1. What destroyed half of the city? _____
2. Who tried to defend the city? _____

3. Where were the ships which were sunk? _____

4. Who commanded the soldiers to leave the city? _____

5. When did the city surrender? _____

Follow-up

F.   Dictation: Write the sentences that your teacher reads aloud.

1. _____

2. _____

3. _____

4. _____

5. _____

G.   Answer the following questions.

1. Who is in command of the military in your country?
2. Has your city ever been bombed? When?
3. When does the military march in parades in your country?
4. Who has the highest rank in the army in your country?
5. How can a war end?
6. What happened to the Titanic?
7. What is above us in this building?
8. Who usually controls the money in families in your country?
9. What things can destroy a building?
10. Would you like to be a sailor? Why or why not?

H.   Describe a war movie which you have seen.

Clothing

Word Form Chart

NOUN	VERB	ADJECTIVE	ADVERB
appropriateness		appropriate	appropriately
inappropriateness		inappropriate	inappropriately
bargain	bargain	bargaining	
belt			
charge	charge		
cloth			
cotton		cotton	
cover	cover	covered	
	uncover	uncovered	
favorite			
fit	fit		
formality		formal	formally
informality		informal	informally
habit		habitual	habitually
material			
		several	
sock			
sweater			
thickness	thicken	thick	thickly
tightness	tighten	tight	tightly
width	widen	wide	widely

Definitions and Examples

1. **belt**

    Most **belts** are made of leather.
    I want to buy a **belt** the same color as my shoes.

2. **bargain** [something that is inexpensive but good]

    If you shop carefully, you can get good **bargains**.

    A: Did you buy that leather belt?
    B: Yes, I did. It was a good **bargain**—beautiful, but not expensive.

3. **fit** [to be the correct size]

    If a shirt is too big, it does not **fit**.

    A: Did those boots **fit** you?
    B: No. They were too big. I wear size nine, but they were size ten.

4. **material** [what something is made of]

    Leather and wool are **materials** that are used to make clothing.
    The **material** of most boots is leather.
    Wood and brick are **materials** that are used to make houses.

5. **cotton** [a material made from the white part of the cotton plant]

    Clothing for warm weather is often made of **cotton**.
    I bought some **cotton** shirts at the store.

6. **sock** [a covering for the foot]

    In warm weather, it is more comfortable not to wear shoes and
       socks.
    What size **socks** do you wear?

7. **cloth** [material made from cotton, wool, etc., usually used to make
    clothing, table covers and many other items]

    Some kinds of **cloth** are of man-made materials.
    This summer shirt is made of light, cotton **cloth**.

8. **cover** [to be on top of, or in front of, something so that you cannot see
    it; to go completely over]

    If curtains **cover** your windows, no one can see into your
       apartment.
    Gloves **cover** your hands and make them warm.
    A blanket **covers** a bed.
    A lid is a **cover** for a pot.

9. **several** [more than two or three, but not many]

My sister owns **several** pairs of shoes but only one pair of boots.

A: Did you buy anything downtown?
B: Yes. I got **several** good bargains—a jacket, some boots, a belt, and a purse.

10. **habit** [something that you usually do]

One of my friends **habitually** buys blue clothes—almost all of her clothing is blue.

A: My husband has some bad **habits**.
B: What does he do?
A: He always puts his dirty clothes on the floor, and he talks in his sleep.

11. **favorite** [the one that you like most]

Red is my **favorite** color. I like red more than all of the other colors.

A: What's your **favorite** type of food?
B: I can't decide. I like Chinese food, but I also like Mexican.

12. **appropriate** (for) [correct; the right type for a place, weather, a person, etc.]

It is not **appropriate** to wear wool clothing in hot weather.
Ideas about **appropriate** clothing are different in different countries.

A: Do you like Kim's dress?
B: Yes. It's beautiful. But it's **inappropriate** for school. She should wear it to a party.

13. **formal** [appropriate for important times and places]

You wear **formal** clothing to important parties, for example, a dinner with the head of your government.
In the United States, **formal** clothing is not appropriate for school.
People rarely wear **formal** clothing on vacation. They usually wear **informal** clothing.

14. **charge** (a) [to make someone pay]

   I go to that store because they **charge** good prices.

   A: What did the clerk **charge** you for that belt?
   B: Twenty dollars.
   A: He was wrong. The correct price is eighteen dollars.

   (b) [to buy something now but pay at another time]

   If you **charge** something at a store, the store sends you a bill the next month.
   Some stores do not permit anyone to **charge** purchases.

   Clerk: This shirt is ten dollars, please.
   Mrs. Brown: I don't have enough money now. May I **charge** it?
   Clerk: Yes. Please write your name and phone number here.

15. **wide** [big from side to side]

   A road with six lanes is **wide**.
   This dress has a **wide** belt.

   A: How big is your room?
   B: It's ten feet **wide** and twenty feet long.

16. **thick** [deep or wide; not thin]

   Winter coats are made of **thick**, heavy material.
   Some wool blankets are **thick**.
   We say that soup is **thick** if it does not have much water. **Thick** mud has a lot of dirt and little water.

17. **tight** [too small; fitting close to the body]

   Tight shoes hurt your feet.
   My belt was too **tight** after I ate a big dinner.

18. **sweater** [clothing worn for warmth on the upper part of the body]

   A warm **sweater** often has lots of wool in it.

   A: It's cold outside.
   B: I know. I'll wear a thick **sweater**.

Introductory Exercises

A.   Match each word with its definition.

    ____   **1.** to be the correct size

    ____   **2.** to make someone pay

    ____   **3.** worn on the foot, but not a shoe

    ____   **4.** what something is made of

    ____   **5.** big from side to side

    ____   **6.** a covering to keep the upper body warm

    ____   **7.** not thin

    ____   **8.** correct

    ____   **9.** something made from cotton or wool or man-made material used for clothing, curtains, etc.

    ____ **10.** more than two or three

    ____ **11.** something that you do often

    ____ **12.** the one that you like best

    ____ **13.** appropriate for important places

    ____ **14.** something that is inexpensive but good

    ____ **15.** close to the body

a. appropriate for
b. bargain
c. belt
d. charge
e. cloth
f. cotton
g. cover
h. favorite
i. fit
j. formal
k. habit
l. material
m. several
n. sock
o. sweater
p. thick
q. tight
r. wide

B.   Say the appropriate word from the word form chart to fill each blank.

1. Leather and cotton are both _____-s for clothing.

2. If you are going to meet a king, you should wear _____ clothes.

3. The music that you prefer is your _____ music.

4. It is not _____ to wear formal clothes to a picnic.

5. Clothes that are the correct size _____ well.

6. If you _____ something at a store, you will receive a bill later.

7. It is a good _____ to exercise every day.

8. If you buy something for a good price, you can say that you got a _____ .

9. If you are very hungry, you might eat _____ sandwiches.

10. You can _____ a dirty wall with paint.

11. Your shoes will hurt if they are too _____ .

12. A road with five lanes is _____ .

13. In cold weather you need a _____ blanket.

14. Strong _____ is good for making a farm worker's clothes.

15. You can wear a _____ over your shirt in winter.

Study Exercises

C. Write **T** if the answer is true and **F** if it is false.

_____ 1. Tight shoes are often too wide.

_____ 2. Formal clothes are appropriate for a farm.

_____ 3. A belt is clothing that covers the hands.

_____ 4. Students who are habitually absent often fail.

_____ 5. Cotton clothing is appropriate for hot weather.

_____ 6. Most people have several houses.

_____ 7. A wide street may have six lanes.

_____ 8. Wool is an appropriate material for a house.

_____ 9. An expensive house that needs many improvements is a bargain.

_____ 10. If your clothes are the right size, they fit well.

_____ 11. People usually like the music of their favorite singer.

_____ 12. You can cover a refrigerator with a pencil.

_____ 13. A tie is formal clothing for a man.

_____ 14. Socks are worn on the hands.

D. Circle the word which is different.

1. cotton	wool	brick
2. thick	wide	tight
3. none	several	many
4. bargain	sell	inexpensive
5. never	usual	habit
6. favorite	prefer	common
7. sock	cloth	sweater

E. Rewrite the following to make correct sentences.

1. appropriate / material / is / summer clothes / cotton / for

   _____

2. was / this / belt / a bargain / wide

   _____

3. breakfast / juice / habitual / bread / and / cheese / my / is

   _____

4. insects / picnic / several / types of / to / came / our

   _____

5. I / for /wool / the winter / thick / bought / a / jacket

   _____

6. charged / too much / this shirt / the clerk / me / for

   _____

7. wear / shoes / don't / I / to / tight / like

   _____

8. that / won't / refrigerator / small / kitchen / fit / my / wide / into

   _____

9. when / went / lost / I / sweater / I / my / to the beach / socks / and

   _____

Follow-up

F. Dictation: Write the sentences that your teacher reads aloud.

1. _____

2. _____

3. _____

4. _____

5. _____

G. Answer the following questions.

1. Where do you wear formal clothing? Informal?
2. What is made of cotton?
3. What is your favorite color? Your favorite food?
4. What clothing is appropriate for a party with your friends?
5. Where in your city can you get clothes at bargain prices?
6. Do you have any bad habits? Tell about one.
7. What can you do when your shoes are too tight?
8. Is anyone near you wearing a belt? Who?
9. What is the width of the room you are in?
10. What covers the windows in your house at night?
11. What material is your house made of?
12. Does your favorite clothing store permit you to charge things?
13. Are there several children in your family? How many?
14. What do you do with clothes that do not fit?
15. When do you wear thick socks?
16. What kinds of material can a sweater be made of?

H. Describe your favorite clothing for formal situations. For informal situations.

Transportation

Word Form Chart

NOUN	VERB	ADJECTIVE	ADVERB	PREPOSITION
accident		accidental	accidentally	
center		central	centrally	
danger	endanger	dangerous	dangerously	
engine				
	flatten	flat		
fuel	fuel			
gasoline				
gas				
happening	happen			
			instead	instead
kind				
leader ⚇	lead (led, led)			
		loud	loudly	
	modernize	modern		
		narrow	narrowly	
		terrible	terribly	

Definitions and Examples

1. **accident** [something that is not expected, usually something bad]

    I **accidentally** hit John with the door when I came in.

    A: Have you ever been injured in a car **accident**?
    B: Yes. I had a bad **accident** last year.

2. **center** [the middle part of a place or thing]

    There will be a big parade in the **center** of town tomorrow.

    A: Do you prefer to live in the **center** of town or in the suburbs?
    B: In the **center** because I don't have a car.

3. **dangerous** [able to hurt a person]

    We cross that **dangerous** intersection every day.

    A: Is Tom a good driver?
    B: No. He drives **dangerously**. He always drives too fast.

4. **fuel** [something used to produce heat or movement]

    You cannot drive a car without **fuel**.

    A: Do airplanes use the same **fuel** as cars?
    B: No. They're **fueled** by something different.

5. **gasoline** [a liquid fuel]

    Gasoline is used as a fuel for trucks and cars.
    The informal way to say **gasoline** is "gas."

    A: Is **gasoline** very expensive in your country?
    B: Yes, because we have to buy it from other countries.

6. **engine** [a machine that uses fuel to make something move or work]

    My car has a big **engine** and can go very fast.

    A: How many **engines** does that train have?
    B: It has two **engines** because it has to pull many cars.

7. **flat** [with no hills or mountains]

    During our vacation we drove through **flat** land. We saw no hills or
    mountains.

    A: Is the land in your country **flat** or mountainous?
    B: It's very **flat** in most places.

8. **instead** (of) [in place of]

    I watched television **instead of** doing my homework.

    A: Did you write a letter to your family last night?
    B: No. I went to the movies **instead**.

9. **kind** [a type]

    There are many **kinds** of cars made in the United States.

    A: What **kind** of gasoline do you use in your car?
    B: The most expensive **kind**. It's better for the car.

10. **lead** (to) (a) [to produce]

> Not studying can **lead to** bad grades.
> Driving too fast in the snow can **lead to** an accident.

(b) [to go]

> A: Where does this street **lead**?
> B: It **leads to** my house.

(c) [to be in charge of]

> Hassan **led** the group of soldiers in the battle.
> All armies need good **leaders**.

11. **loud** [noisy; not quiet]

> Many young people like to listen to **loud** music.
> Most people do not like **loud** noise.

> A: What's wrong?
> B: That **loud** noise frightened me.

12. **modern** [new; of the present time]

> Many **modern** cars are small.

> A: Do you like **modern** music?
> B: No. It's too loud.

13. **narrow** [not wide]

> The streets in the old part of the city are **narrow**. The ones in the
> modern part of the city are wide.

> A: Are the beds on the train comfortable?
> B: No. They're hard and **narrow**.

14. **happen** [to be]

> A: Where did the accident **happen**?
> B: It **happened** near that dangerous intersection in the center of
> town.

15. **terrible** [very bad; horrible]

> There was a **terrible** train accident last year in my country. Ten
> people died, and many more people were injured.

> A: Did your family go to the movies last night?
> B: Yes. We saw a **terrible** movie that frightened the children.

Introductory Exercises

A. Match each word with its definition.

     ____ **1.** very bad   **a.** accident

     ____ **2.** a type   **b.** center

     ____ **3.** new   **c.** engine

     ____ **4.** not quiet   **d.** fuel

     ____ **5.** something bad that can happen   **e.** happen

     ____ **6.** to show the way   **f.** instead of

     ____ **7.** a machine that makes cars   **g.** kind
                 and trucks move   **h.** lead

     ____ **8.** not wide   **i.** loud

     ____ **9.** something used to produce heat   **j.** modern
                 or make machines work.   **k.** narrow

     ____ **10.** the middle part of a place or thing   **l.** terrible

B. Answer each question with a word from the word form chart in this
unit.

1. What is something bad that can happen to people in cars, trucks,
   airplanes, etc.?
2. What is the name of the machine in your car that makes it move?
3. Which word describes a very bad accident?
4. Which verb means to take you some place?
5. What kinds of cars are made today?
6. Which word describes the noise that a helicopter makes?
7. What do you put into your car engine to make it move?
8. What do engines and machines need to work?

Study Exercises

C. Match the words that have similar meanings.

     ____ **1.** fuel   **a.** middle

     ____ **2.** machine   **b.** gasoline

     ____ **3.** center   **c.** horrible

     ____ **4.** terrible   **d.** engine

D. Match the words that have opposite meanings.

_____ **1.** modern   **a.** wide
_____ **2.** narrow   **b.** good
_____ **3.** terrible   **c.** quiet
_____ **4.** loud   **d.** old

E. Write **T** if the sentence is true and **F** if it is false.

_____ **1.** Driving dangerously can lead to an accident.
_____ **2.** You can drive a car without fuel.
_____ **3.** There are many hills on flat land.
_____ **4.** Fast drivers are dangerous.
_____ **5.** When you blow the horn in your car, it makes a loud noise.
_____ **6.** Bicycles have engines.
_____ **7.** If you drive in the center of the road you might have an accident.
_____ **8.** Gasoline is a kind of fuel.

F. In the blanks, write the appropriate word(s) from the word form chart in this unit.

1. Government offices are usually in the _____ of town.
2. Young men like cars with big _____ -s .
3. Driving too fast can _____ to an _____ .
4. The noise that an airplane makes is _____ .
5. Many houses in the city are old, but the houses in the suburbs are more _____ .
6. Mary decided to buy a blue car _____ of a red one.
7. The accident _____ -ed at the airport last year.
8. The streets in the old part of the city are too _____ for big trucks.
9. A good _____ helps teams to win games.

G. Read the dialogue and answer the questions that follow.

Anna: I saw a terrible accident last night.
Beverly: Where did it happen?
Anna: On North Street.
Beverly: Isn't North Street that narrow street that leads to the busy intersection in the center of town?
Anna: Yes. The accident happened near the modern office building at that intersection.
Beverly: Was anyone injured?
Anna: Well, a car was hit by a fuel truck carrying gasoline. An ambulance took both drivers to the hospital.
Beverly: Why did the accident happen?
Anna: I think the man in the car was driving dangerously. He was driving too fast, and he couldn't stop when he saw the fuel truck.
Beverly: What kind of car was he driving?
Anna: A big one with a big engine. In a smaller car, maybe he could have stopped in time.

Write **T** if the sentence is true and **F** if it is false.

_____ **1.** Anna saw a terrible accident last week.

_____ **2.** North Street is a wide street that leads to the center of town.

_____ **3.** The fuel truck was carrying gasoline.

_____ **4.** The accident happened because the driver of the car was driving dangerously.

_____ **5.** The driver of the car stopped when he saw the truck.

_____ **6.** The man's car had a big engine.

Follow-up

H. Dictation: Write the sentence that your teacher reads aloud.

1. _____

2. _____

3. _____

4. _____

5. _____

I.   Answer the following questions.

1. Are there many modern buildings in the city where you live? Where?
2. Are there many car accidents in your country? Why or why not?
3. What kinds of transportation do you use to go from one country to another?
4. How much does gasoline cost in your country?
5. Is there much flat land in your country? Where is it located?
6. What do you do sometimes instead of doing your homework?
7. Are most of the streets in your city wide or narrow?
8. Do you drive dangerously? Why or why not?
9. What kinds of modern machines can you use?
10. What is your favorite kind of car? Why?

J.   Describe one of the following:

a. A terrible accident in which someone was injured.
b. The kinds of modern cars that you like best.
c. Loud noises that you do not like.

Government

Word Form Chart

NOUN	VERB	ADJECTIVE	ADVERB	PREPOSITION
				according to
capital		capital		
comment	comment			
commentary				
commentator ⚲				
constitution		constitutional	constitutionally	
constitutionality				
democracy		democratic	democratically	
election	elect	elected		
	generalize	general	generally	
information	inform	informed		
		informational		
		international	internationally	
official ⚲		official	officially	
order	order	orderly		
		ordered		
responsibility		responsible	responsibly	
symbol	symbolize	symbolic	symbolically	
vote	vote	voting		
voter ⚲				
wish	wish	wishful	wishfully	

Definitions and Examples

1. **according** (to) [as spoken or written by]

   According to the newspaper, 300 soldiers were killed by bombs last week.

   Student A: How many people speak Spanish in the United States?
   Student B: **According to** my professor, about eight million people.

2. **capital** [the city where the government of a country or state is located]

   Washington, D.C. is the **capital** of the United States.

   A: What's the **capital** of Peru?
   B: Lima—it's the largest city in Peru, too.

3. **comment** (on) [to give an opinion; to say something about a subject]

   Newspapers often **comment on** the president's speeches.
   My teacher **commented** that my paper was the best in the class.
   On the TV news last night, the president made a **comment on** the attack on the embassy.

4. **constitution** [a plan of laws of a country, which says how the country will be governed]

   The **constitution** of the United States was written in 1789.
   According to the **constitution**, a person must be born in the United States to be president.
   When a new country is born, the government often writes a **constitution**.

5. **vote** (for, on) [to make a decision, usually a public decision, about a person who will be in the government or about a law]

   Children are not permitted to **vote**.

   A: Did you **vote for** Adams for student president?
   B: No. I think Adams is lazy. I **voted for** Smith.

   We are going to **vote on** her idea tomorrow.

6. **elect** [to choose (usually a person in the government) by voting]

   American **elect** a new president every four years, and each president may be **elected** only two times.
   The high school baseball team **elected** a new leader last month.
   The person who receives the most votes in an **election** is the winner.

7. **general** [about everyone or everything; about the main idea or parts of something]

> The president made only **general** comments in his speech. He gave no examples.
>
> The **general** public is permitted to enter some rooms in the White House, but not the private areas.
>
> A: What is the **general** idea of an ambassador's job?
>
> B: **In general** an ambassador's job is to help the people of one country understand the people of another country.

8 **inform** [to tell someone about something]

> The teacher **informed** the students that they were going to have a test the next day.
>
> A president uses newspapers, radio, and television to **inform** people about new government plans.
>
> People get **information** about government from books, newspapers, television, and from other people.

9. **international** [about people or things from many different countries]

> Many **international** students study at this university; there are students from China, Saudi Arabia, and France.
>
> An **international** company, such as Phillips, has offices in many countries.
>
> Radio and television allow us to hear about **international** news a short time after it occurs.

10. **official** [someone who can command other people or who has control over a school, government, office, etc.]

> School **officials** must make decisions about changes in school classes, books, and programs.
>
> The airport **official** closed the airport because of fog.
>
> A: There was a lot of snow today. How did you come to school?
>
> B: The road near my house was **officially** closed, but many people were using it.

11. **democracy** [a government in which people govern themselves through elected officials]

> In a **democracy** the people elect officials who decide the laws of the country.
>
> The United States is a **democratic** country.
>
> A: If the people in a **democracy** don't like the president, what do they do?
>
> B: They don't elect him again.

12.   **order** (a) [to command]

> When there is an emergency, the police often **order** people to stay indoors.
>
> The president **ordered** the government officials to do a study of agriculture in the country.

(b) [in a restaurant, to ask for food or drink]

> Waitress: May I take your **order**?
> Customer: Yes. I'd like soup and a salad, please.

13.   **responsible** [having control over decisions]

> Parents are **responsible** for their children; they must give their children food, clothes, and love.
>
> Newsman: Mr. President, who will be **responsible** for the new employment program?
> Mr. President: Ms. Smith, a lawyer from California, will be the head of the new program.

15.   **symbol** [a letter, picture, animal, etc. that means something else]

> The **symbol** for "gold" is Au.
> The sign ♡ may **symbolize** love.
>
> A: What does the **symbol** ☮ mean?
> B: It was a **symbol** for peace in the 1960's. A white bird is also a **symbol** for peace.

16.   **wish** [to want]

> I **wish** I could take a trip this summer, but I do not have enough money.
>
> In a democracy, the government officials must listen to the **wishes** of the people.

Introductory Exercises

A. Match each word with its definition.

_____ **1.** to command
_____ **2.** to choose by voting
_____ **3.** a letter or picture that means something else
_____ **4.** as spoken or written by someone
_____ **5.** to want
_____ **6.** the head city of a state or country
_____ **7.** a plan for the laws of a country
_____ **8.** about many countries
_____ **9.** to tell someone about something
_____ **10.** to give an opinion about something

a. according to
b. capital
c. comment
d. constitution
e. democracy
f. elect
g. inform
h. international
i. official
j. order
k. responsible
l. symbol
m. vote
n. wish

B. Answer **TRUE** or **FALSE**.

1. The head of a democracy is a king.
2. Students can elect their teachers.
3. The capital of the United Kingdom is London.
4. Parents are responsible for the needs of their children.
5. Americans choose a new constitution every four years.
6. An international company hires employees from different countries.
7. The symbol for a dollar is $.
8. People should vote for irresponsible officials.
9. A constitution is a person who heads a government.
10. You comment on a book when you inform someone about the book.
11. A book with exact explanations of one idea is not general.
12. Most countries have several capitals.

Study Exercises

C. In the blanks, write the appropriate word(s) from the word form chart on this unit.

1. "I want to _____ you about the new driving law," said the policeman to his audience.

2. What does the color green _____ in your country?

3. The _____ at the airport wanted to see my passport.

4. Students are _____ for doing their homework on time.

5. I _____-ed a glass of milk and a sandwich for lunch today.

6. The government employees _____-ed that the government would raise their salaries. They have not had a raise in two years.

7. Whom did you _____ for in the last presidential election?

8. In a _____ , the people elect the head of the government and most of the officials.

9. The _____ public in the United States wants peace with the Soviet Union.

10. The teacher gave me good _____-s on my paper about the war in Ireland.

11. Employees of an _____ company should speak several languages.

12. The head of the government usually lives in the _____ city of the country.

13. _____ to a new book about international employment, the level of education of government officials is improving.

D. Write the correct preposition(s) after each word.

1. inform (someone) _____   for
2. vote _____   about
                                                on
3. comment_____

4. responsible _____

E. Read the passage and answer the questions that follow.

Sally McBride is a high school student. Her school is doing an international study about countries in Africa and Asia. She is interviewing the ambassador from X, a country in Africa.

5 McBride: Mr. Ambassador, last year your country wrote a new constitution. Would you please give me your comments on this?

Ambassador: Yes. I would be happy to. According to the new constitution, members of the government will

10   be democratically elected by all the people. We
     will hold general elections every six years.
McBride: Will women be allowed to vote?
Ambassador: Yes. Everyone's vote will be important.
McBride: Where is the official home of the president?
15 Ambassador: The official home of our new president is in
     the capital city although his private home is in
     his hometown, 500 miles east of the capital.
McBride: What do you feel is the president's most
     important responsibility to the people of your
20   country?
Ambassador: His first responsibility is to follow the wishes
     of the people. And to do that, he must build
     the country's education and job programs. I
     think he will succeed. He has ordered, for
25   example, that twenty new schools be built in
     areas outside of the capital.
McBride: What will these schools mean for the people?
Ambassador: The schools symbolize the president's promise
     to help all of the country, not only the people
30   who live in the capital.
McBride: Thank you, Mr. Ambassador. My school wishes
     you success.

1. When did country X write a new constitution? _____

_____

2. How often will they elect new government members? _____

_____

3. Will only men be allowed to vote? _____

_____

4. Where does the president officially live? _____

_____

5. What do the new schools symbolize? _____

_____

Follow-up

F.   Dictation: Write the sentence that your teacher reads aloud.

1. _____

2. _____

3. _____

4. _____

5. _____

G.   Listen to the definitions. Say the word from the word form chart in this unit that matches the definition.

1. the city with a country's government offices
2. an opinion spoken or written about a subject
3. the time when people choose a president by voting
4. ideas and plans that you tell or give other people
5. a government in which the people elect officials
6. having the ability to control decisions
7. to want
8. with people from many countries
9. something that means something else
10. a plan of the laws of a country

H.   Answer the following questions.

1. Does your country have a constitution?
2. Who is responsible for education in your country?
3. What is the symbol of your country? Of the United States?
4. What is the capital city of your country?
5. Are there elections in your country? How often?
6. How old do you have to be to vote?
7. What is the official language of your country?
8. Are there international students in your school?
9. Where do you get information about your government?
10. Who in your family gives orders?

Banking

Word Form Chart

NOUN	VERB	ADJECTIVE	ADVERB
account			
addition	add	additional	additionally
borrower ⚲	borrow	borrowed	
cash	cash		
coin			
count	count	counted	
		counting	
earnings	earn	earned	
earner ⚲			
		special	especially
		exact	exactly
interest			
lender (⚲)	lend (lent, lent)	lending	
multiple	multiply	multiple	
multiplication			
penny			
quarter			
total	total	total	totally

Definitions and Examples

1. **penny** [a one-cent piece of money]

    You cannot buy many things with only a **penny**.
    The clerk gave her a dollar for her 100 **pennies**.

2. **quarter** [a 25-cent piece of money]

You have to use **quarters** in that public telephone.

A: Do you have four **quarters** for a dollar?
B: Sure. Here you are.

3. **coin** [a piece of hard money]

Pennies and quarters are **coins**.
Dollars are usually not **coins**.
Coins are not paper money.

4. **total** [all of something]

The **total** of 50 and 25 is 75.
I have a **total** of $1,000 in the bank.

5. **cash** [paper money and coins]

It is dangerous to carry a lot of **cash** in your pocket; someone might
    steal it.
In some stores, you must pay **cash** for your purchases; in others you
    can charge your purchases.

6. **add** [to put things together; to put more of something]

If you **add** two and two, you get four.
Children learn how to **add** numbers in elementary school.
I need some **additional** money to pay for the gift for the teacher.

7. **interest** [money which a bank pays you each month because you have
put money in the bank; when you borrow money, the additional
money you must pay]

I chose that bank because it pays high **interest**.
He borrowed some money, and now he is having trouble because of
    the high **interest** he has to pay.

8. **earn** [to receive money from a job or from interest]

My money is **earning** interest in the bank.

A: How much does he **earn** per year?
B: He has a good job; he **earns** $80,000 a year.

9. **especially** [very]

That bank is paying **especially** high interest now.
The weather here is **especially** nice in the spring.

10. **exact** [having no errors]

> People who work in banks must be careful to be **exact**.
> His salary last year was **exactly** $30,000.

11. **multiply** [to increase; to add a number to itself as many times as another, given number]

> Two **multiplied** by three is six: $2 \times 3 = 6$.
> Children learn **multiplication** in school after they learn addition.

12. **count** (a) [to work with numbers, usually adding them]

> Clerks in stores must **count** money carefully.

> (b) [to say numbers in order]

> The little boy could **count** only to ten.

13. **borrow** [to get money or something else from someone and have to return it later]

> When you need money, sometimes you can **borrow** it from a friend.
> When people buy a house, they often **borrow** money from a bank.

14. **lend** [to give someone money or something else to use and to expect to have it returned later]

> Banks often **lend** money to people who need it.

> A: Can you **lend** me a dollar? I forgot my wallet.
> B: Sure.

15. **account** [a place in a bank to put money]

> Some types of bank **accounts** pay interest; others do not.
> She has a lot of money in her bank **account**.

> A: Which bank do you have your **account** with?
> B: The City Bank.

16. **special** [not usual; very nice]

> My birthday is always a **special** day for me.
> That bank has **special** accounts for children.

Introductory Exercises

A. Match each word with its definition.

_____ 1. to put things together

_____ 2. to give someone money to use for a time

_____ 3. a one-cent piece of money

_____ 4. very

_____ 5. a place in a bank to put money

_____ 6. a piece of hard money

_____ 7. all of something

_____ 8. a 25-cent piece of money

_____ 9. to receive money from a job or interest

_____ 10. paper money and coins

_____ 11. having no errors

_____ 12. not usual; very nice

a. account
b. add
c. borrow
d. cash
e. coin
f. count
g. earn
h. especially
i. exact
j. interest
k. lend
l. multiply
m. penny
n. quarter
o. special
p. total

B. Complete each sentence with a word from the word form chart in this unit.

1. You have to pay the taxi driver in _____ .

2. I get _____ on that bank account.

3. Pennies and quarters are _____ -s .

4. When I needed money, I _____ -ed some.

5. How much does he _____ each year for that job?

6. The bank will _____ you money to build a house.

7. It's 90° F today. That's _____ hot for June.

8. The clerk carefully _____ -ed the money I gave him.

9. 10 + 10 = 20 is an example of _____ .

10. 10 × 10 = 100 is an example of _____ .

Study Exercises

C. Write **T** if the sentence is true and **F** if it is false.

_____ **1.** Banks often lend money to people.

_____ **2.** Most people want high earnings.

_____ **3.** Children learn multiplication before they learn addition.

_____ **4.** Ten multiplied by twenty is exactly 200.

_____ **5.** Carrying a lot of cash is not dangerous.

_____ **6.** The total of 10 and 10 is 21.

_____ **7.** All bank accounts pay interest.

_____ **8.** People like to pay interest to banks.

_____ **9.** One-year-old children can count to 100.

_____ **10.** If something is special, you can find it everywhere.

D. Write sentences with the words.

1. my / money / put / an account / in / I

_____

2. earns / each / he / $3,000 / month

_____

3. my / counted / they / carefully / the bank / at / money

_____

4. interest / month / account / that / from / I / get / each

_____

5. borrowed / a bank / money / from / they

_____

6. total / in / the exact / is / $1,200 / account / my

_____

E.   Read the passage and answer the questions that follow.

When Mary graduated from high school, she decided to
open a bank account. In addition to the money for college
which her father gave her, she had a job on campus. Her
earnings from her campus job were not much, but she did
5   not want to keep the cash in her dorm room. She also knew
that she might want to borrow money in the future and that
banks like to lend money to people who have accounts with
them.

So Mary made telephone calls to the banks near the
10   campus to find out which ones paid the highest interest.
After learning exactly how much interest her account could
earn at each bank, she chose to open an account at the
Winter Bank. They paid high interest, and they had a special
type of account for university students; with this special
15   account, students could borrow up to $200 at any time and
pay only low interest on the borrowed money.

1. What did Mary decide to do when she graduated from high school?

_____

2. Did Mary earn a lot from her campus job? _____

_____

3. What did Mary not want to have in her dorm room? _____

_____

4. Whom do banks like to lend money to? _____

_____

5. Why did Mary call the banks near the campus? _____

_____

6. What two advantages did the Winter Bank have?

(1) _____

(2) _____

Follow-up

F. Dictation: Write the sentences that your teacher reads aloud.

1. _____

2. _____

3. _____

4. _____

5. _____

G. Answer the following questions about your country.

1. How much does a doctor earn each year? A teacher?
2. Why do people borrow money from banks?
3. Do banks pay interest? How much?
4. Do people carry cash? Is it dangerous?
5. When do children learn addition? Multiplication?
6. Other than banks, who lends people money?
7. Do people make most of their purchases with cash?
8. Which kind of account do you especially like? Why?
9. After people make a purchase in a store, do they count the change that the clerk gives them?

H. Explain why people choose a bank. What makes one bank better than another?

Farming

Word Form Chart

NOUN	VERB	ADJECTIVE	ADVERB
agriculture		agricultural	agriculturally
cattle			
century			
crop			
excess	exceed	excessive	excessively
		excess	
flood	flood	flooded	
hay			
lack	lack		
market	market	marketable	
		marketed	
		marketing	
peasant ⚐			
purpose			purposely
		purposeful	purposefully
		rural	
seed			
share	share	shared	
		sharing	
supply	supply	supplied	
		supplying	

Definitions and Examples

1. **agriculture** [the science of raising food or animals]

   Agriculture is very important in that country.
   They make most of their money through **agriculture**.
   He did not like working in **agriculture**; he decided to leave the farm
   and move to the city.

2. **cattle** [cows raised for meat]

   They own the largest **cattle** ranch in this area.
   The ranchers sold a lot of **cattle** to that company.
   Cattle that eat corn usually produce better meat.

3. **lack** [not to have or not to have enough]

   They **lack** the money they need to buy more cattle.
   That family **lacks** nothing; they have everything they need and
   more.

4. **century** [one hundred years]

   Our family has owned this farm for more than a **century**.
   Many people moved from the farms to the cities at the beginning of
   this **century**.
   Two **centuries** ago most people in that area were farmers, but now
   they own stores.

5. **crop** [many plants grown by someone]

   The most important **crops** from that farm are wheat, corn, and
   apples.
   The farmers lost their **crop** because of the dry weather.

6. **excess** [more than necessary]

   The farmers had an **excess** of wheat, so they had to sell it at a
   lower price.
   A: What will you do with the **excess** apples?
   B: I'll divide them among my family and my brother's and sister's
   families.

7. **excessive** [too much; so much that it is bad]

   The student's absences were **excessive**; he failed the course.

8. **hay** [dried grass that is used to feed animals]

   That field is used only for growing **hay**.
   The cattle eat **hay** and corn.
   Farmers usually store **hay** in the top part of a barn.

9. **market** [a place to buy and sell crops or other products]

> They took the cattle to **market**.
> The **market** price went up, so everyone wanted to sell.

10. **peasant** [a poor farmer who works on and owns little or no land]

> Centuries ago in Europe, the **peasants** worked most of the farmlands.
> Most **peasants** work hard for little money.

11. **purpose** [the reason for doing something]

> He works hard for the **purpose** of taking care of his family.
>
> A: What is the **purpose** of growing so much hay?
> B: Well, we will use part of it to feed the cattle now. We will store another part until winter and will sell what is left.

12. **rural** [in the farm or country area]

> We like living in the city but go on picnics in the **rural** areas.
> The air in the **rural** areas smells fresh and clean.
> There are many farms in the **rural** areas of this country.

13. **seed** [the small, hard part of a plant from which new plants grow]

> The farmer planted the fields with **seeds** this morning.
> Farmers must prevent hungry birds from eating the **seeds** that they plant.
> **Seeds** require water to grow into plants.

14. **flood** [to have too much water on the land]

> It rained all week, and the rivers rose and **flooded** the town.
> Because that area is so low, the river **floods** it every spring.
> The **flood** destroyed all the farmer's crops.

15. **share** (with) [to give part of what you have to someone]

> When the flood destroyed our house, our neighbors **shared** their house and food **with** us.
> Farmers often **share** their crops **with** each other.
> Members of a farming family **share** many responsibilities.

16. **supply** (with) [to fill a need]

> The farmers **supplied** us **with** information on growing crops.
> These two ranches **supply** the area **with** most of its meat.
> Our company **supplies** people to help with the excess work on farms.

Introductory Exercises

A. Match each word with its definition.

    ____ **1.** to give part of   **a.** agriculture

    ____ **2.** to have too much water on the land   **b.** cattle

    ____ **3.** one hundred years   **c.** century

    ____ **4.** what plants grow from   **d.** crops

    ____ **5.** in the country area   **e.** flood

    ____ **6.** what farmers raise   **f.** hay

    ____ **7.** cows raised for meat   **g.** lack

    ____ **8.** farming   **h.** peasant

    ____ **9.** not to have   **i.** rural

    ____ **10.** grass for animal food   **j.** seed

                                       k. share

                                       l. supply

B. Answer **TRUE** or **FALSE**.

1. Cattle are raised for their meat.
2. People eat hay in salads.
3. A century is ten years.
4. A flood is when too much water comes onto land.
5. Rural areas have a lot of traffic and noise.
6. The purpose of agriculture is building cars.
7. Seeds are important in agriculture.
8. Peasants live in the rural areas.
9. If you have an excess of money, you lack money.
10. When people share, they give things to other people.

Study Exercises

C. In the blanks, write the appropriate word(s) from the word form chart.

1. If you like farming, you should study _____ .
2. If you like quiet, you should live in a _____ area.
3. If you want to grow plants, you need some _____-s .
4. If your cows are hungry, you can feed them _____ .
5. If you have more than enough, you have an _____ .
6. If the river rises too high, there will be a _____ .
7. _____-s are people, usually poor people, who work in rural areas.

8. If you do not have enough, you _____ what you need.

9. Why you do something is called your _____ .

10. If a farmer has excess crops, he can _____ them with his neighbors.

D. Circle the word which is different.

1. seed   plant   cattle

2. peasant   crop   farmer

3. farm   rural   century

4. cattle   horses   flood

5. crop   excess   enough

6. share   flood   supply

E. Use the definitions, examples, or descriptions to fill in the blanks.

ACROSS

1. poor country farm worker
3. something farmers grow
4. too much of something
5. having too little of something
7. what plants grow from
9. growing food
10. to fill a need
12. to give part of

DOWN

1. why someone does something
2. the science of farming
6. one hundred years
8. grass for animals to eat
9. destructive water
11. cows raised for meat

F. Read the passage and answer the questions that follow.

Two centuries ago this city was nothing but farms. The area was famous for agriculture. It was important in people's lives, and there were many peasant farmers. They grew many crops, but they always had an excess of corn and wheat. They
5 usually sold this excess in the local markets, but often they would share their excess crops with their neighbors.

These peasant farmers also supplied the local towns with most of their meat. The peasants raised cattle and used some of their corn crop to feed them. They also grew hay for the
10 purpose of feeding their animals.

1. What was this city many years ago? _____

How long ago? _____

2. What did the farmers grow? _____

_____

3. What did the farmers do with their excess crops? _____

_____

4. What else did the peasants supply to the town? _____

_____

5. What did the farmers feed their animals? _____

_____

Follow-up

G. Dictation: Write the sentences that your teacher reads aloud.

1. _____

2. _____

3. _____

4. _____

5. _____

H. Put the expressions in each group in time order. Which comes first? second? third?

Group 1: flood, destroy area, rain excessively

1. _____

2. _____

3. _____

Group 2: supply food, plant seeds, prepare fields, grow crops

1. _____

2. _____

3. _____

4. _____

Group 3: feed animals, cut hay, supply meat, grow hay

1. _____

2. _____

3. _____

4. _____

I. Answer the following questions.

1. Is agriculture important in your country? In what areas is agriculture most common?
2. What are the most important crops in your country?
3. Who does most of the farming?
4. Whom do the farmers sell their crops to? Where do they sell them?
5. Are floods a problem in your country? In what areas? What problems are there? What can the people do to prevent flooding?
6. What do the peasants in the rural areas lack? What are their most important needs?
7. Do the farmers in your country share anything? What?
8. Have you ever lived on a farm? Visited a farm? What type of farm was it?

Sports

Word Form Chart

NOUN	VERB	ADJECTIVE	ADVERB
basketball			
		certain	certainly
contest	contest	contested	
contestant ⚥		contesting	
fall	fall	fallen	
		falling	
individual ⚥	individualize	individual	individually
jump	jump	jumping	
kick	kick	kicking	
lift	lift		
nature		natural	naturally
race	race	racing	
score	score	scoring	
soccer			
strength	strengthen	strong	strongly
superiority		superior	
talent		talented	

Definitions and Examples

1. **contest** [a game or competition]

    When those two teams play, it is always an exciting **contest**.

    A: What do you think the game will be like?
    B: Well, I see it as a **contest** between a big team and a fast team.

2. **basketball**

    Young people often play **basketball** indoors during the winter.

    A: Where did you learn to play **basketball**?
    B: In school.

3. **certain** [known to be true; sure]

    My team is **certain** to win.
    The game **certainly** was exciting.

    A: I know we're going to win tonight.
    B: How can you be so **certain**?

4. **fall** [to go accidentally to the ground or the floor]

    One player lost the ball and **fell** to the floor.

    A: What happened to her?
    B: She **fell** down. She's all right.

5. **lift** [to use the arms to raise something off the ground]

    When George fell down, the other players **lifted** him and carried
        him to the side.

    A: This box is heavy.
    B: Let me help you **lift** it.

6. **individual** [a person]

    Individuals have to work with each other.
    It was an **individual** effort, not a team effort.

7. **individually** [related to each person separately]

    A: Did you talk to the team about their loss?
    B: Yes. I talked to each member of the team **individually**.

8. **jump** [to use your legs to push yourself up off the ground]

    Basketball players have to **jump** high off the floor.

    A: Do you think he'll be able to play with the team?
    B: Maybe. He's not very tall, but he can **jump** well.

9. **kick** [to use the feet to hit something or someone]

    Basketball players may not **kick** the ball.
    The child hurt his brother when he **kicked** the ball at him.

    A: What happened to your leg?
    B: Somebody **kicked** me during the game.

10. **natural** [not made by people]

Wood is a **natural** product. Glass is not.

A: I want to learn to play like that.
B: She's got **natural** skill. It's not something you can learn.

11. **talent** [a high level of skill]

The best players have a lot of natural **talent**.

A: Do you think I have **talent**?
B: Not for basketball. Your **talent** is for learning English words!

12. **race** [to run fast in competition with other people]

Two players **raced** after the ball.

A: It was a **race**, and I won.
B: But you didn't get the ball.

13. **score** (a) [in some sports, to put the ball into the other team's defended area]

Their team **scored** three times in one minute.

(b) [the number your team receives when you score]

A: What's the **score**?
B: 65 to 61.

14. **soccer** [a game in which the players kick the ball on a field]

Soccer is the most commonly played sport in the world.

A: In my country people play football.
B: In the United States, it's called **soccer**. The Americans say "football" for a different kind of ball game.

15. **strength** [how much force something or someone has]

You need a lot of **strength** to play basketball well.

A: The team has no great players.
B: Yes, but they have **strength** and experience.

16. **superior** [better]

The **superior** team will usually win.

A: I think our team is **superior** in defense.
B: Maybe.

Introductory Exercises

A. Match each word with its definition.

____ 1. a game in which players kick the ball	**a.** basketball
____ 2. to use your legs to push yourself up off the ground	**b.** certain
	c. contest
	d. fall
____ 3. known to be true	**e.** individual
____ 4. to run fast in competition with others	**f.** jump
	g. kick
____ 5. how much force something has	**h.** lift
____ 6. to use your arms to raise something up	**i.** natural
	j. race
	k. score
____ 7. a game or competition	**l.** soccer
____ 8. not made by people	**m.** strength
____ 9. one person	**n.** superior
____ 10. to use your foot to hit something	**o.** talent

B. Say the appropriate word from the word form chart.

1. One person is an _____ .

2. A game which is frequently played indoors is _____ .

3. The players running up the floor are _____ -ing for the ball.

4. She can play basketball well. She has a lot of _____ .

5. To throw the ball over their heads you have to _____ up off the floor.

6. The score is 75 to 45. We are _____ to win.

7. We won 75 to 45. We have the _____ team.

8. In basketball you are not allowed to _____ the ball.

9. One sport in which you can kick the ball is _____ .

Study Exercises

C. Write **T** if the sentence is true and **F** if it is false.

_____ **1.** Soccer is a sport in which you throw the ball to score.

_____ **2.** Strength is not an advantage in basketball.

_____ **3.** Soccer is usually played outdoors.

_____ **4.** Fans usually like to watch a superior team.

_____ **5.** Individual sports are different from team sports.

_____ **6.** The superior team usually wins.

_____ **7.** To play basketball you need to be able to kick the ball well.

_____ **8.** Basketball is a competitive sport.

_____ **9.** Natural talent can be learned from a good teacher.

_____ **10.** The score is 50 to 50. We won!

D. Write sentences with the words.

1. exciting / basketball / a good / is / game

_____

2. some / play / people / indoors / soccer

_____

3. won / because of / they / strength / their superior / the game

_____

4. she / to get / jumped / the ball / high

_____

5. to win / they / this game / certain / are

_____

6. game / the soccer / he / scored in

_____

7. this exciting / was / the final / contest / score / of / 66 to 65

_____

E. Circle the word which is different.

1. basketball   soccer   talent
2. group   team   individual
3. superior   indoors   outdoors
4. contest   competition   team
5. fall   jump   lift
6. game   contest   weak
7. natural   score   win

F. Read the passage and answer the questions that follow.

         Basketball is a very common sport in the United States. It can be played indoors or outdoors at any time of year. But it is usually played indoors during the winter when it is too cold to play other sports outdoors. High school, university,
5 and professional teams have exciting contests, and fans come to see great talent and skill.
         In some ways, basketball is like soccer. Both sports use a large ball. They are played on a field or floor, and they are fast-moving. In both, scores are made by putting the ball into
10 the other team's defended area.
         There are, of course, differences. In scoring, for example, basketball players use their hands to throw the ball. Soccer players can score by kicking the ball or by hitting it with some other part of their body or head, but they cannot throw
15 the ball for a score. Soccer teams also move the ball by kicking it. Basketball players are not allowed to move the ball with their feet. They must use their hands. They can also throw the ball to other players. It is necessary for them to be able to jump high for the ball and throw it high. For
20 this reason, good basketball players are usually very tall.

1. When is basketball usually played in the United States? Where? ____

_____

2. How is basketball like soccer? _____

_____

3. How do you move the ball in basketball? In soccer? _____

_____

4. Why are basketball players tall? _____

_____

Follow-up

G. Dictation: Write the sentences that your teacher reads aloud.

1. _____

2. _____

3. _____

4. _____

5. _____

H. Answer the following questions.

1. Is basketball played in your country? If yes, is it indoors or outdoors? At what time of year?
2. What sport is most commonly played in your country?
3. What sport do people most like to watch?
4. Are there teams in the high schools and universities? For which sports?
5. Are there professional teams? For which sports?
6. What sport do you like to watch most? Why?
7. Which sport do you have the most talent for?
8. Do you prefer individual or team sports? Why?

I. Tell a story about the following situation. What will happen?

John is at home on school vacation. He's bored. He finds a large old ball in his bedroom.

Weather and Geography

Word Form Chart

NOUN	VERB	ADJECTIVE	ADVERB	PREPOSITION
		Celsius		
		centigrade		
degree				
equator		equatorial		
		Fahrenheit		
	freeze	frozen		
		freezing		
gas		gaseous		
liquid		liquid		
measurement	measure	measured		
		measuring		
	melt	melted		
		melting		
			perhaps	
season		seasonal	seasonally	
solid	solidify	solid		
temperature				
thermometer				
tropics		tropical		
type		typical	typically	
				under

Definitions and Examples

1. **temperature** [how hot or cold something, someone, or someplace is]

   The **temperature** in the summer is high.
   When the **temperature** is low, you should wear more clothes.
   His **temperature** was high because he was sick and had a fever.

2. **liquid** [water, milk, and juice are liquids]

   It is good for your health to drink a lot of **liquids**.
   The sick man could eat only **liquid** foods.

3. **gas** [not a solid and not a liquid]*

   We breathe **gases**.
   There are solid fuels, liquid fuels, and **gaseous** fuels.

4. **solid** [not liquid or gas]

   Ice and wood are **solids**.
   Something which is **solid** is hard when you feel it.
   That table is heavy because it is made of **solid** wood.

5. **season** [a time of the year; spring, summer, fall, and winter]

   During the rainy **season** in my country, it rains every day.

   A: Which **season** do you like best?
   B: Spring, I think.

6. **typical** [common; usual; being like others of the same kind]

   A **typical** spring day in New York is rainy.
   It is **typical** to have snow in Moscow in January.

7. **melt** [to become liquid from being solid]

   The snow **melts** in the spring when the weather gets warm.
   The ice in my Coke slowly **melted**.

8. **freeze** [to become solid from being liquid, because of cold]

   We **freeze** some foods to make them last longer.
   The rain **froze** and turned into ice on the roads.

---

*For an additional meaning of **gas**, see Volume 1, Unit 12.

9. **measure** [to learn how large, how hot, or how heavy something is, usually with an instrument]

> The clerk **measured** the weight of the package with a scale. He also **measured** its length and width.

10. **thermometer** [a small instrument for measuring temperature]

> The nurse put a **thermometer** in the patient's mouth to take his temperature.
>
> I looked at the **thermometer** outside my kitchen window to see if I needed to wear a coat.

11. **degree** [a measure of temperature]

> **degree** Fahrenheit [a temperature measurement used in the United States]
>
> **degree** Celsius = degree centigrade [a temperature measurement]
>
> Zero **degrees** Celsius (or centigrade) (0° C) is the same as 32 **degrees** Fahrenheit (32° F)
>
> Water boils at 100 **degrees** Celsius (or centigrade) (100° C) and at 212 **degrees** Fahrenheit (212° F)

12. **perhaps** [maybe]

> **Perhaps** tomorrow will be sunny, but I don't think so.
>
> A: Do you think it will be colder soon?
> B: **Perhaps**, but it's still only early fall.

13. **equator** [a line around a map of the earth between the northern half and the southern half]

> Countries which lie on the **equator** have hot weather all year.
> The ship crossed the **equator** during the night.

14. **tropics** [the areas of the earth near the equator]

> People in the **tropics** wear light clothing because of the heat.
> The weather is very **tropical** there; you will not need your coat.

15. **under** (a) [less than]

> I always wear a coat if the temperature is **under** 60° F.

(b) [in a place less high than]

> You can put a small suitcase **under** your seat on the plane.
> In this picture, the X is **under** the line: _____
>
> X

Introductory Exercises

A. Match each word with its definition.

_____ **1.** an instrument for measuring temperature

_____ **2.** to become liquid from being solid

_____ **3.** a time of the year

_____ **4.** common; usual

_____ **5.** how hot or cold something is

_____ **6.** maybe

_____ **7.** in a place less high than

_____ **8.** a line around a map of the earth between the northern and southern halves

_____ **9.** to become solid from being liquid

_____ **10.** to use an instrument to judge how large something is

_____ **11.** water, milk, and juice are examples of this

_____ **12.** not a solid and not a liquid

a. centigrade
b. degree
c. equator
d. freeze
e. gas
f. liquid
g. measure
h. melt
i. perhaps
j. season
k. seasonally
l. temperature
m. thermometer
n. typical
o. under

B. Complete each sentence with a word from the word form chart in this unit.

1. The tropical areas of the earth are near the _____ .

2. Winter, spring, summer, and fall are _____ -s .

3. Zero degrees Celsius is a cold _____ .

4. When water freezes, it becomes _____ .

5. To measure temperature, you use a _____ .

6. The areas near the equator are _____ .

7. When snow melts, it becomes _____ .

8. The measurement of temperature that is typical in the United States is degrees _____ .

9. Another word meaning 'maybe' is _____ .

10. When the weather gets warm, the snow _____ -s .

Study Exercises

C. Write **T** if the sentence is true and **F** if it is false.

_____ **1.** Water freezes at 100° C.

_____ **2.** England is in the tropics.

_____ **3.** You use a thermometer to measure temperature.

_____ **4.** The sun does not shine very much at the equator.

_____ **5.** If something is typical, you can find other examples of it.

_____ **6.** People everywhere use degrees Fahrenheit.

_____ **7.** People in tropical places often use fans.

_____ **8.** You use a scale to measure weight.

_____ **9.** If X is under Y, then Y is higher than X.

_____ **10.** People drink solids.

_____ **11.** Water is a gas.

D. In the blanks, write the appropriate word(s) from the word form chart in this unit.

1. I looked at the _____ to see the temperature.

2. That was a _____ summer day, exactly like most summer days.

3. Because those countries lie near the _____ , they have very hot weather.

4. The highest temperature yesterday was eighteen _____-s Celsius.

5. Liquids _____ when they are very cold.

6. If the sun shines all day, some of the snow will _____ .

7. _____ it will snow tomorrow; I do not know.

8. A thermometer _____-s temperature.

9. When the temperature is _____ zero degrees Celsius, water freezes.

10. People drink _____-s .

11. If you heat a liquid, it will become a _____ .

E. Read the passage and answer the questions that follow.

Three years ago, John took a trip around the world by ship. Of course, he saw many unusual things during his trip, which lasted for six months. But the experience that he had when the ship crossed the equator was perhaps the strangest
5 experience for him
The ship had been in the tropics for several days, and everyone had been very quiet because of the heat: the temperature had not been under 85° Fahrenheit for two days. John had gone to his room to rest during the afternoon.
10 Unexpectly, two workers on the ship came to his room and asked him if he had crossed the equator before. When John said, "No," they made him come with them, saying that they were going to a party. When they arrived at the place on the ship where the other passengers and crew were waiting, John
15 was surprised to be hit with lots and lots of sea water. Everyone was laughing, and they told him that this was a typical "party" for people crossing the equator for the first time.

1. Where was the ship when John had his strange experience? _____

_____

2. Why had the people on the ship become quiet? _____

_____

3. What did the crew members ask John? _____

_____

4. Why was John hit with sea water? _____

_____

Follow-up

F. Dictation: Write the sentences which your teacher reads aloud.

1. _____

2. _____

3. _____

    4. _____

    5. _____

G. Answer the following questions.

    1. How high does the temperature typically get in your country in the summer? How low in the winter?

    2. Have you been in a tropical country? Where?

    3. Have you crossed the equator? Was there anything unusual about the experience?

    4. What is the weather forecast for tomorrow?

    5. Do the rivers in your country freeze sometimes? When?

    6. During which season do visitors like to come to your country? Why?

    7. What is a typical weather forecast for a winter day in your city? For a summer day?

H. Describe your favorite season in your country.

Environment

Word Form Chart

NOUN	VERB	ADJECTIVE	ADVERB
cause	cause	causal	causally
environment		environmental	environmentally
	float	floating	
forest		forested	
forestry			
invention	invent	inventive	inventively
inventor ⚲			
leak	leak	leaking	
		leaky	
		major	
method		methodical	methodically
oil		oily	
pollution	pollute	polluted	
present		present	presently
result	result	resulting	
smoke	smoke	smoky	
sufficiency		sufficient	sufficiently
insufficiency		insufficient	insufficiently
world		worldwide	

Definitions and Examples

1. **world** [the earth]

   There are more than 100 countries in the **world**.
   He took a trip around the **world**.

2. **environment** [the world around us and the living things in it]

   We should be careful not to hurt our **environment**.

   A: What type of **environment** do you like?
   B: I like to be in the country, with a lot of trees.

3. **pollution** [something that makes the environment dirty]

   Pollution is a big problem now in many parts of the world.

   A: What **polluted** this river?
   B: That factory.

4. **smoke** [the dirty air from a fire]

   The **smoke** from that factory pollutes the air.
   Smoky air hurts my eyes.

5. **method** [a way to do something]

   We need a **method** to control the smoke from that factory.
   As part of that **method** of language teaching, the students repeat
   each word many times.

6. **oil** [a liquid fuel that is found underground]

   The Middle Eastern countries produce a lot of **oil**.
   That factory uses **oil** as its fuel.

7. **present** (a) [now; at this time]

   The **present** problem with pollution in this area is very bad.
   Presently the government is investigating the problem; they may
   find the answer soon.

   (b) [in a short time; soon]

   I will answer your question **presently**.

8. **forest** [an area with many trees]

   Many animals live in the **forest**.
   Forest fires are very dangerous.

9. **major** [big; important]

  A **major** forest fire kills a lot of animals and destroys many trees.

  A: What is the **major** crop in your country?
  B: Rice.

10. **cause** [to make something be]

  Factories often **cause** pollution.
  Wars **cause** many deaths.

  A: What is the **cause** of the problem?
  B: We don't know.

11. **float** [to stay on the top of a liquid]

  Oil **floats** on water.
  If a ship does not **float**, it will sink.

12. **invent** [to make a new machine or a new method]

  We must **invent** a method to clean polluted water so that we can drink it.
  Inventors need to have many new ideas.

13. **leak** [when a liquid, by accident, gets out of the thing it should be in]

  The oil which **leaked** out of the ship floated on top of the sea.

  A: Did you find the **leak**?
  B: No. I don't know where the liquid came from.

14. **sufficient** [enough]

  Many countries do not have **sufficient** clean water.
  When people do not have **sufficient** fuel, they take the wood from the forests.

15. **result** [something that is caused by something else]

  The **result** of his hard work was clear: the business was doing very well.
  The growth in the number of factories has **resulted** in more pollution in this area.

Introductory Exercises

A. Match each word with its definition.

_____ **1.** the dirty air from a fire	**a.** cause
_____ **2.** an area with many trees	**b.** environment
_____ **3.** a liquid fuel that is found underground	**c.** float
_____ **4.** to make something be	**d.** forest
_____ **5.** to make a new machine or method	**e.** invent
_____ **6.** now; at this time	**f.** leak
_____ **7.** a way to do something	**g.** major
_____ **8.** to stay on top of a liquid	**h.** method
_____ **9.** the Earth	**i.** oil
_____ **10.** the world around us and the living things in it	**j.** pollution
_____ **11.** enough	**k.** present
_____ **12.** something that makes the environment dirty	**l.** result
	m. smoke
	n. sufficient
	o. world

B. Complete each sentence with an appropriate word from the word form chart in this unit.

1. The fuel that many factories use is _____ .

2. We can't use this pot. It has a _____ .

3. Oil stays on top of water because it _____ -s .

4. This water is not good to drink because it is _____ -d .

5. A way to do something is a _____ .

6. A fire produces _____ .

7. Many animals live in the _____ .

8. At first we didn't know how the fire started, but now we know its

_____ .

9. We have a lot of food for the party; it should be _____ .

Study Exercises

C.   Write **T** if the sentence is true and **F** if it is false.

_____ **1.** If a ship leaks, it may sink.

_____ **2.** People need insufficient food to live.

_____ **3.** Some countries are part of the world and some are not.

_____ **4.** Pollution has a good result.

_____ **5.** If you live near a forest, it is part of your environment.

_____ **6.** Wood floats.

_____ **7.** Oily water is good to drink.

_____ **8.** Doctors want to know the causes of diseases.

_____ **9.** An inventive person has many ideas.

_____ **10.** Something which is worldwide is found in only a few places.

_____ **11.** People worry about major problems.

_____ **12.** People like methods with good results.

D.   Match the words that have opposite meanings.

_____ **1.** cause   **a.** hold
_____ **2.** float   **b.** clean
                                                c. sink
_____ **3.** insufficient   **d.** small
_____ **4.** leak   **e.** result
                                                f. cause
_____ **5.** major   **g.** enough
_____ **6.** polluted   **h.** past
_____ **7.** present

_____ **8.** result

E.   Read the passage and answer the questions that follow.

   One month ago, a major accident happened to a large
ship that was carrying oil to the east coast of the United
States. The oil leaked from the ship and polluted the water
and the areas near where the accident happened.
5   The owners of the ship quickly attempted to get help in
controlling the floating oil. They contracted with a company
called Clean Ocean Company, which said that it had
invented a method to clean up floating oil. Because the result
of such oil leaks is major environmental pollution, many
10 companies have been working on such an invention, but not

very successfully. However, the Clean Ocean Company
declared their invention to be a success.

    Unfortunately, they were not able to control the oil, and
it reached the beaches two days later. Presently, the
15 government is spending a lot of money attempting to clean
up the coast, but they predict that the pollution will cause
the deaths of many birds and fish before the clean-up is
completed.

1. What was the ship carrying? _____

_____

2. What was polluted? _____

_____

3. Why did the ship's owner hire the Clean Ocean Company? _____

_____

4. Why have many companies been working on oil control inventions?

_____

_____

5. How do we know that the Clean Ocean Company's method was not

successful? _____

_____

6. What does the government think will be the result of this pollution?

_____

_____

Follow-up

F.   Dictation: Write the sentences that your teacher reads aloud.

    1. _____

    2. _____

    3. _____

4. _____

5. _____

G.   Answer the following questions.

1. What are the major causes of air pollution in your city?
2. Does your country have much forest land? Where?
3. Name a famous inventor. What did he or she invent?
4. Describe the methods used to control pollution in your country.
5. Was the environment in your country better in the past than the present? Explain.
6. Does your country produce oil? How much?
7. Does your country have sufficient laws about polluting the environment? What other laws are needed?
8. Which are the most polluted cities in the world?
9. Is the air in your city smoky? Why?

H.   Describe the major environmental pollution problems in your country. What is being done to stop these problems?

Media

Word Form Chart

NOUN	VERB	ADJECTIVE	ADVERB
advertisement	advertise	advertised	
ad			
advertiser (人)		advertising	
advertising			
article			
author 人	author		
belief	believe	believable	believably
disbelief		unbelievable	unbelievably
		current	currently
fact		factual	factually
headline	headline	headlined	
media (plural)			
medium (singular)			
paragraph	paragraph	paragraphed	
print	print	printed	
printing		printing	
publication	publish	published	
		publishing	
publisher (人)			
sentence			
title	title	titled	
	entitle		
topic		topical	topically
translation	translate	translated	
translator 人			

Definitions and Examples

1. **media** [ways of public communication]

    Newspapers, radio, television, and magazines are all examples of **media**.

    A: Did you hear the president's speech about the **media**?
    B: Yes. He doesn't trust them. He thinks that they aren't giving correct information about his programs.

2. **article** [a piece of writing in a newspaper or magazine]

    The most important **articles** in a newspaper are usually on the first page.
    Magazine **articles** are often longer than newspaper **articles**.

    A: Did you see the **article** about agricultural problems in yesterday's paper?
    B: The one about the lack of seed and supplies? Yes, I did.

3. **author** [the person who wrote a book, article, song, etc.]

    The **authors** of this book are Dorolyn Smith, Holly Rogerson, Linda Schmandt, and Gary Esarey.
    Shakespeare was the **author** of many English comedies.

4. **title** [the name of a book, article, song, etc.]

    Das Kapital is the **title** of a famous book by Karl Marx.
    Time and Newsweek are **titles** of internationally-known magazines in English.

5. **believe** [to think that something is true, without knowing that it is certain; to have an opinion]

    The author of this article does not **believe** in eating meat. He writes that we should eat only vegetables.
    The man's excuse was not **believable**, so the judge sent him to jail.

    A: Which team do you think will win the game?
    B: Oh, I **believe** the North will win. They have the best defense.

6. **topic** [the subject of an article, book, speech, etc.]

    The **topic** of this newspaper article is the environment. It is about methods of controlling pollution.

    A: What was the **topic** of the meeting yesterday?
    B: We talked about gasoline and oil prices.

7. **print** [to use a machine to put words or pictures on paper; to make something available for the public to read]

> Newspapers **print** local, national, and international news.
> "The **print** media" means newspapers, magazines, and books, but not radio or television.

8. **headline** [the title of a newspaper article]

> A **headline** is usually printed in large letters.
> The front page **headline** in yesterday's paper was ATTACK ON U.S. EMBASSY.

9. **publish** [to print something for the public to read]

> In most cities, a newspaper is **published** every day; in a small town, there is sometimes only a weekly paper.

> A: What does your brother do?
> B: He's a **publisher**. His company prints books and sells them in Asia.

10. **current** [from or about the present time]

> The media give us information about things that are **currently** happening.
> Because of improvements in international media, **current** news is available almost everywhere.

11. **fact** [a piece of information that everyone knows is true]

> These are **facts**: The earth is round.
> There are 50 states in the United States.
> John F. Kennedy was killed in 1963.
> Newspapers print both **facts** and opinions.

12. **advertisement** {informal: **ad**} [words and/or pictures, usually published, for the purpose of selling something]

> I read an **ad** in the school paper about a bicycle for sale.
> This store is **advertising** televisions at bargain prices.
> I will never buy that magazine again because its **advertisements** are horrible.

13. **translate** [to change word meanings from one language to another]

> You can use a dictionary to **translate** these words.
> When the heads of two countries meet, they often need **translators** to help them understand each other.

14. **sentence** [a group of words that begins with a big letter and ends with . or ? or !]

> A **sentence** must have a subject and a verb in English.
> This is a **sentence**.
> A **sentence** with the symbol ? at the end is a question.

15. **paragraph** [a group of sentences about one topic]

> The first sentence of a **paragraph** usually says what the topic will be.
> My assignment last night was to write a **paragraph** of 200 words about my current job.

Introductory Exercises

A. Match each word with its definition.

_____ 1. to change word meaning from one language to another

_____ 2. a group of words that begins with a big letter

_____ 3. to print for public sale

_____ 4. about the present time

_____ 5. to think something is true; to have an opinion

_____ 6. a subject

_____ 7. the title of a newspaper article

_____ 8. to put words on paper with a machine

_____ 9. a person who writes something

_____ 10. the name of a book or article

_____ 11. a group of sentences about one topic

_____ 12. ways of public communication

a. advertisement
b. article
c. author
d. believe
e. current
f. fact
g. headline
h. media
i. paragraph
j. print
k. publish
l. sentence
m. title
n. topic
o. translate

B. Answer each question with a word from the word form chart in this unit.

1. What do you call a person who writes books?
2. I want to sell my car. What can I put in the newspaper to help me?
3. What do you call a story in a newspaper?

4. What do you need if you don't understand a language?
5. What is usually in big letters on the front page of a newspaper?
6. What are radio, television, books, magazines, and newspapers?
7. What short piece of writing has many sentences but only one general idea?
8. What do you call the name of a song or story?
9. Who prints a newspaper or a book?
10. What word can you use when you think something is true?
11. What is another word for the subject of a book or article?

Study Exercises

C. Write **T** if the sentence is true and **F** if it is false.

_____ 1. A fact is something that people believe without being certain about it.

_____ 2. The title of this book is Words for Students of English.

_____ 3. The topic of this book is English vocabulary.

_____ 4. This book has several authors.

_____ 5. There are usually many advertisements in a newspaper article.

_____ 6. The media often publish current information.

_____ 7. An opinion is the same as a fact.

_____ 8. There are ten sentences in this exercise.

_____ 9. An author writes about many different ideas in a paragraph.

_____ 10. Headlines are usually printed in small letters.

_____ 11. To translate an article, you must know two languages.

_____ 12. The purpose of an advertisement is usually to sell something.

D. In the blanks, write the appropriate word(s) from the word form chart in this unit.

1. Newspapers usually _____ a lot of articles about crime and other problems.

2. I watched my favorite news program last night; the _____ of the program was "Can You Trust the Media?"

3. I'm learning two foreign languages because I want to become a _____ .

4. Five hundred years ago, most people _____-d the world was flat.

5. Is it a _____ that most children do not like school, or is it only your opinion?

6. The peace group wanted to tell the public their opinion about the president's plan, so they bought an _____ in a major newspaper.

7. In some places the government decides which information the newspapers should _____ .

8. We had to read an article about current environmental problems. The first few _____-s were about the causes of pollution.

E.   Circle the word which is different.

1. author   writer   article
2. print   entitle   publish
3. title   headline   translation
4. sentence   media   paragraph
5. question   story   article
6. opinion   belief   fact

F.   Read the passage and answer the questions that follow.

There was an interview on TV yesterday with Ken Ackerman, the author of a book about the media. The topic of the book is the growing importance of the media in our lives. Ackerman says that almost everyone hears the radio
5   news or reads a newspaper every day. Even people who do not have much time read the headlines and a few sentences or paragraphs on the front page of the paper. People who are interested in international topics might buy a paper printed in New York, London, or another big city. These papers
10   usually have the most current information.
Ackerman believes that the media have too much control over our ideas. Advertisers promise to improve our lives with a new car or cleaning product, and people believe the ads. People often accept an opinion that they read in the
15   newspaper. "If it's printed," they think, "it must be true." They forget that not everything that is published is factual.
The interview with Ackerman was very interesting. The title of his book is <u>The Modern Media</u>, and it is published by a Canadian company. The book is currently available in local
20   bookstores.

1. What is Ken Ackerman's profession? _____

_____

2. What is his book about? _____

_____

3. According to Ackerman, are newspaper articles always completely

   true? _____

_____

4. Why do many people believe the promises and opinions in

   newspapers? _____

_____

5. What is the name of Ackerman's book? _____

   Can you buy it now? _____

6. Write the first sentence of the last paragraph in this reading passage.

_____

_____

Follow-up

G. Dictation: Write the sentences that your teacher reads aloud.

1. _____

2. _____

3. _____

4. _____

5. _____

H. Listen to the definitions. Say the word from this unit that matches the definition.

1. the person who wrote a published article
2. the title of a newspaper article
3. the subject of a book
4. to change from one language into another
5. a group of sentences with one idea
6. to think that something is true
7. a news story in a magazine
8. to write with a machine
9. ways of public communication
10. published words or pictures to sell something
11. to print for sale
12. information that everyone accepts as true

I. Answer the following questions.

1. What is the title of your favorite book? Who is the author? What is the topic?
2. Translate the sentences in number 10 below into your language.
3. How many newspapers are available in your town? How often are they published? Are the publishers local or in another city?
4. What is the headline on the front page of today's paper?
5. Do you prefer to read articles that are only factual, or do you like to know the author's opinion? Why?
6. Which type of media do you usually get current news from?
7. What is the most important topic that is currently in the news in your country?
8. Do you believe everything in the newspaper? Why or why not?
9. Do you believe that the media should print information about the private lives of famous people? Why or why not?
10. Tell about an advertisement that you believe. Tell about one that you don't believe.

Nature

Word Form Chart

NOUN	VERB	ADJECTIVE	ADVERB
		afraid	
		unafraid	
fear	fear	fearful	fearfully
		fearless	fearlessly
discovery	discover	discovered	
exploration	explore	explored	
		exploring	
explorer ⚹			
flow	flow	flowing	
leaf (leaves)		leafy	
path			
pleasure		pleasurable	pleasurably
		pleasant	pleasantly
		unpleasant	unpleasantly
pond			
rock		rocky	
sand		sandy	
scene		scenic	
scenery			
snake			
zoo			

Definitions and Examples

1. **discover** [to find something new]

    Children in the United States learn that Christopher Columbus **discovered** America.

    A: Oh look! I **discovered** a beautiful bird in the garden!
    B: What a nice **discovery**.

2. **leaf** {plural: **leaves**} [the green parts of a tree]

    Leaves can be large or small.

    A: Do we have to clean up all of these **leaves** today?
    B: Yes. Soon all of the **leaves** will fall off the trees.
    A: I hate fall!

3. **pond** [a small pool of water]

    This farm has a **pond**.

    A: Are there any fish in the **pond**?
    B: Yes, but only a few because it's so small.

4. **rock** [a stone]

    In the mountains there are many **rocks**.

    A: I live in a **rocky** area.
    B: You must live near the mountains.

5. **path** [a narrow place to walk]

    This **path** leads to the pond, and the other **path** leads into the forest.

    A: I don't like that part of the park. There are no **paths** there.
    B: OK. We can walk here on the good **path**.

6. **sand** [the very, very, small pieces of rock found in deserts and beaches]

    I live in a **sandy** area.

    A: Do you have **sand** near your home?
    B: Oh yes! I live in the desert. **Sand** is everywhere!

7. **scenery** [natural things to look at in an area; for example: ponds, beaches, mountains, trees]

    The **scenery** in the mountains is very beautiful.

    A: Look at the **scenery** outside the window.
    B: This is a great apartment!

8. **snake**

   Snakes have no legs.

   A: Look at the **snakes**!
   B: Oh no! I don't like **snakes**.

9. **fear** [to be scared]

   Many people **fear** snakes.
   I **fear** flying in airplanes.

10. **afraid** [scared]

    A: Do you like mountain climbing?
    B: No. I'm **afraid** of high places.

11. **explore** [to look for things in a new place]

    Explorers discover new places.

    A: Will you **explore** the rocky path with me?
    B: OK. I've never gone there before.

12. **zoo** [a place made by people to see many animals]

    There are usually many jungle animals in the **zoo**.

    A: Can we go to the **zoo** today?
    B: Good idea. I hear they have some new animals.

13. **flow** [to move in one direction, usually used to describe water]

    The Nile River **flows** north.

    A: Which way does the river **flow**?
    B: It **flows** south, and it **flows** very quickly.

14. **pleasant** [nice]

    This path is very cool and **pleasant**.

    A: I like Maria. She's a **pleasant** person.
    B: Yes. She's always laughing and smiling.

Introductory Exercises

A. Match each word with its definition.

_____ 1. pleasant   **a.** discover

_____ 2. the small green parts of a tree   **b.** fear

                                          c. flow

_____ 3. to find something   **d.** leaves

_____ 4. a narrow place to walk   **e.** nice

                                          f. path

_____ 5. a place to see animals   **g.** rock

_____ 6. a stone   **h.** sand

_____ 7. deserts and beaches have lots of this   **i.** scenery

                                          j. zoo

_____ 8. natural things seen in an area

B. Answer each question with a word from the word form chart.

1. Where is a place to see interesting animals?
2. Which part of a tree is small and green?
3. How do you feel if you are scared?
4. How does a river move?
5. Where can you walk in a forest?
6. What kind of person may discover new places?
7. What kind of person is always very nice?
8. What animal is long and thin?

Study Exercises

C. Write **T** if the answer is true and **F** if it is false.

_____ 1. Many people are afraid of rocks.

_____ 2. A pond may freeze in the winter.

_____ 3. Explorers sometimes make important discoveries.

_____ 4. It is pleasant to live in a place with beautiful scenery.

_____ 5. A zoo is a place to swim.

_____ 6. A river may flow from the mountains to the ocean.

_____ 7. Snakes are tall, fat animals.

_____ 8. Deserts are sandy.

D.   Match each word with the word or phrase closely associated with it.

____ **1.** sand	**a.** afraid
____ **2.** fear	**b.** desert
____ **3.** pleasant	**c.** find
____ **4.** leaf	**d.** look for
____ **5.** explore	**e.** movement
____ **6.** rock	**f.** nice
____ **7.** discover	**g.** river
____ **8.** path	**h.** stone
	i. street
	j. tree

E.   In the blanks, write the appropriate words from the word form chart in this unit.

        Last week, Bob and Carolyn had nothing to do, so they went for a walk. They wanted to (1) _____ new places and to (2) _____ things in these new places. First, they walked down a narrow (3) _____ . Walking was cool because there were many (4) _____ trees on the path. When they got near the (5) _____ , they decided to take a swim, and later they sat on a (6) _____ in the sun to get dry. Suddenly, they saw a large (7) _____ on the rock! Carolyn was scared, but Bob was not (8) _____ . He took a stone and threw it at the snake's head. The snake crawled away. They had something exciting to tell their friends.

Follow-up

F.   Dictation: Write the sentences that your teacher reads aloud.

1. _____

2. _____

3. _____

4. _____

5. _____

G. Answer the following questions.

1. Do you like to explore? What kinds of places?
2. Have you ever made a discovery? What and where?
3. What are you afraid of?
4. Do plants grow better in sandy places or rocky places? Why?
5. Do you like to walk on the grass or on a path?
6. Have you ever been to a zoo? What is your favorite animal?
7. What kind of scenery do you like best?
8. What kind of work do you find unpleasant?

H. 1. Describe your visit to a zoo or a park.
2. Describe the scenery in your country.
3. Describe a pleasant place.

Education (B)

Word Form Chart

NOUN	VERB	ADJECTIVE	ADVERB
basics		basic	basically
biology		biological	biologically
biologist 㣨			
chemistry		chemical	chemically
chemist 㣨			
engineering	engineer	engineering	
engineer 㣨			
history		historical	historically
historian 㣨			
		incorrect	incorrectly
intelligence		intelligent	intelligently
junior 㣨		junior	
major (㣨)	major	major	
mathematics		mathematical	mathematically
math			
mathematician 㣨			
perfection	perfect	perfect	perfectly
science		scientific	scientifically
scientist 㣨			
seat	seat	seated	
		seating	
senior 㣨		senior	
undergraduate 㣨			

Definitions and Examples

1. **basic** [at the beginning level]

   I studied **basic** German before I studied advanced German.

   Student A: What classes are you taking this semester?
   Student B: I'm taking **basic** writing and advanced Spanish.

2. **biology** [the study of living things; how plants and animals grow and live]

   The students studied insects and fish in their **biology** class.
   A **biologist** wants to know how plants eat and breathe.

3. **chemistry** [the study of materials to see what they are made of and how they change]

   The students in the **chemistry** class wanted to find out what water is made of.
   The **chemical** symbol for salt is "NaC1."

4. **science** [information about nature, people, and the world, that comes from facts; also laws to explain the facts]

   Biology, chemistry, and mathematics are different types of **sciences**.
   A good school should have a good **science** program.
   Scientific investigations are necessary to find new cures for diseases.

5. **engineering** [the profession that uses scientific information to help in building houses, roads, machines, and other things]

   The student from Africa studied **engineering** to learn the best way to build roads.
   An electrical **engineer** is investigating ways to improve the machines that make electricity.

6. **history** [the study of what has happened in the past]

   People from Europe have been very important in the **history** of the United States.
   There have been two World Wars in modern **history**.
   The students studied the **history** of England from 1750–1880.

7. **incorrect** [wrong]

   An **incorrect** address on a letter means the letter will not arrive.
   The clerk in the store gave me **incorrect** change yesterday.

   Teacher: When did Mexico become free from Spain?
   Student: 1815.
   Teacher: No. Your answer is **incorrect**. The correct answer is 1810.

8. **intelligent** [able to learn and understand well and fast]

> The child was very **intelligent**. He could read when he was three years old.
>
> An **intelligent** person can learn very fast.

9. **junior** [a student in the year before the last year of high school or university]

> High school students in their **junior** year study American history and chemistry.
>
> John stopped studying when he was a **junior** in college because he did not like school. He did not finish the last year.

10. **major** (in) [to study many courses in college in the subject most important for the student's degree]

> When a person **majors in** a subject, he takes courses mostly in that subject.
>
> I **majored in** Spanish at the university and then got a job in Spain.
>
> A: What's your **major**?
> B: Engineering. What's yours?
> A: My **major** is chemistry.

11. **mathematics** {informal: **math**} [the study of numbers and the relations between them]

> In **mathematics** classes in elementary school, students learn to multiply.
>
> It is necessary to understand some **mathematics** before you can study engineering.
>
> Pythagoras was a famous **mathematician**.

12. **perfect** [without mistakes]

> The student wrote a **perfect** composition; there were no errors.
> It is difficult to speak a foreign language **perfectly**.
> My math teacher always expects **perfect** homework.

13. **seat** [the place where someone sits]

> Some students like to sit in the same **seat** every day.
> My favorite **seat** in a restaurant is near a window.
>
> Customer: I'd like a **seat** near the door, please.
> Restaurant manager: Yes. We can **seat** you here to the right of the door.
> Customer: That's fine.

14. **senior** [a student in the last year of high school or university]

   Students graduate at the end of their **senior** year.
   Students should begin to look for jobs when they are **seniors** in college.

   A: What did you take when you were a **senior**?
   B: Advanced French, math, and history.

15. **undergraduate** [a student with no degree studying in a four-year university program]

   Undergraduates must choose a major during their second year in the university.
   Most **undergraduate** programs are four years, but a few programs are five years.

   A: What did you major in when you were an **undergraduate**?
   B: Biology. I wanted to enter medical school after I graduated.

Introductory Exercises

A. Match each word with its definition.

_____ 1. a student in the last year of college
_____ 2. the study of numbers
_____ 3. without mistakes
_____ 4. a place where you sit
_____ 5. the study of plants and animals
_____ 6. a student's most important subject in college
_____ 7. able to learn and understand easily
_____ 8. using science to build machines and roads
_____ 9. a college student who has not yet graduated
_____ 10. the study of the past

   a. basic
   b. biology
   c. chemistry
   d. engineering
   e. history
   f. intelligent
   g. junior
   h. major
   i. mathematics
   j. perfect
   k. seat
   l. senior
   m. undergraduate

B. Answer each question with a word from the word form chart in this unit.

   1. If you are in your fourth year at the university, what are you?
   2. If you study numbers, what do you study?

3. How can you describe a test that has no mistakes?
4. What is your profession if you build bridges?
5. On what do you sit in class?
6. If you do something wrongly, how do you do it?
7. What do you do when you study one subject more than others at college?
8. What is a class at the beginning level?
9. If you study animals, what do you study?
10. What do you call someone who is studying in a four-year college?

Study Exercises

C.   Write **T** if the sentence is true and **F** if it is false.

_____ 1. An engineer must know mathematics.

_____ 2. An undergraduate is someone who has graduated from college.

_____ 3. Intelligence comes from studying hard.

_____ 4. A biologist studies rocks and sand.

_____ 5. A senior has completed three years of college.

_____ 6. A perfect student is often late for class and rarely does homework.

_____ 7. The study of science is important for a good education.

_____ 8. If you want to work for an oil company, you should major in history.

D.   In the blanks, write the appropriate word(s) from the word form chart in this unit.

1. After I studied French at college for two years, I went to France to study during my _____ year.

2. John is very _____ ; he always gets good grades, but he never studies.

3. José has never studied English so must take a _____ English course before he can begin his studies at an American university.

4. My sister _____-ed in mathematics in college.

5. Before students study medicine, they must study _____ and _____ .

6. Your answer, 247, is _____ . The right answer is 243, not 247.

7. The _____ of the United States begins with the arrival of Christopher Columbus in the New World.

8. My _____ in class was in front of the teacher's desk.

E. Write sentences with the words.

1. went / Peru / year / during / to / John / junior / his

_____

2. my / the official / name / incorrectly / spelled

_____

3. to study / I / engineering / wanted

_____

4. like / mathematics / don't / I

_____

5. like / historical / on TV / my parents / programs / to watch

_____

6. major / chemistry / was / his / undergraduate

_____

7. to be / Susan / a biologist / wants

_____

F. Read the passage and answer the questions that follow.

When Sara was a young girl in school, her favorite class was science. She did not like history or art, but she was excellent in mathematics. In high school she also studied chemistry and biology. She was an intelligent girl, and she
5 put a lot of effort into her homework. She always got the best grades in the class, but she was not satisfied with her tests if they were not perfect.

Sara went to the local university, but she could not decide if she wanted to major in chemistry or mathematics.
10 In her first year as an undergraduate, she discovered a field that allowed her to study both—chemical engineering. She studied the basics of engineering in her first two years, and in her junior and senior years she took all the advanced courses.

During her senior year, she received a job offer from a large
15 chemical company. Sara is now a successful chemical
engineer, and she is finally satisfied with her work.

1. What was Sara's favorite class? _____

_____

2. What did Sara study in high school? _____

_____

3. Why did Sara get the best grades in her class? _____

_____

4. Why did Sara major in chemical engineering? _____

_____

5. What did she study in her first two years as an undergraduate? ____

_____

6. When did she receive her job offer? _____

_____

Follow-up

G. Dictation: Write the sentences that your teacher reads aloud.

1. _____

2. _____

3. _____

4. _____

5. _____

H. Answer the following questions.

1. What science classes do you study in high schools in your country?
2. How old are you when you are a senior in your schools?

3. How many years did you study mathematics in your high school?
4. How many years do undergraduates study in your country?
5. Name a famous scientist in your country.
6. What is the most important date in your country's history?
7. What do you wish you could do perfectly?
8. Where is the best seat in a theater?

I.   Tell a story about the following situation. What will happen?

David is in his first year at the university. He wants to be an engineering major, but he failed mathematics the first semester.

Work (B)

Word Form Chart

NOUN	VERB	ADJECTIVE	ADVERB
cooperation	cooperate	cooperative	cooperatively
		uncooperative	uncooperatively
efficiency		efficient	efficiently
inefficiency		inefficient	inefficiently
expert 人		expert	expertly
industry		industrial	industrially
	industrialize	industrialized	
			nowadays
obviousness		obvious	obviously
possibility		possible	possibly
		impossible	impossibly
	quit		
		similar	similarly
		sure	surely
		unsure	
			together
tool			
training	train	trained	
trainer 人			
unemployment		unemployed	
wage			

Definitions and Examples

1. **expert** [a person who does something very well]

   We respect his skill because he is an **expert** at his work.
   To hire an **expert**, we will need to pay a high salary.

2. **wage** [the money paid for each hour of work]

   The **wages** at that factory are very low.

   A: What **wages** does that company pay its part-time employees?
   B: They start at five dollars an hour.

3. **train** [to educate for a job]

   That company **trains** all its new employees for three months.

   A: How much **training** is required for the job?
   B: Only one month.

4. **together** [with someone]

   The boss and her secretary went to the meeting **together**.
   The owner of the company likes his staff to work well **together**.

5. **cooperate** [to work together to do something]

   A nurse has to **cooperate** with the doctor.
   Bosses like employees who are **cooperative**.
   Cooperation is important when people are working in the same
     office.

6. **quit** [to stop working for an employer; to leave a job; to stop doing
   something]

   The wages were so low that I **quit** the job.
   We had to hire a new person because one of our employees **quit**.

7. **tool** [something used to do a job; often, something used by hand to do
   a job]

   I get afraid when I see my dentist's **tools**.
   During the training, I learned to use the **tools** necessary for the job.

8. **efficient** [able to work fast and well]

   The boss likes **efficient** employees.
   That factory produces a lot of cars because it is very **efficient**.
   Old factories are sometimes **inefficient**.

9. **obvious** [very clear; easy to see]

> We saw her work, and it was **obvious** that she was an expert.
> There was an **obvious** problem at the factory; no one was working.

10. **possible** [able to be done; able to happen]

> It is **possible** that the owner will sell the factory soon; he may sell it.
> If something is **possible**, it may happen, but it may not happen.

11. **unemployed** [without a job]

> Many **unemployed** people come to the factory to ask for jobs.
> Sometimes **unemployed** people receive money from the government.

12. **similar** (to) [not the same, but not totally different]

> The work of a nurse is **similar to** the work of a doctor.
> A helicopter and an airplane are **similar**. They are both kinds of transportation by air.

13. **sure** (about) (to) [certain]

> That expert is **sure to** receive a high salary.
> I am not **sure about** her ambition. I think she wants to become a doctor.

14. **nowadays** [now, at this time]

> **Nowadays**, a nurse must have a license, but a long time ago, no license was necessary.
> In the past I ran every day, but **nowadays** I do not get much exercise.

15. **industry** [a business that produces large numbers of things to sell]

> The **industries** in Japan are very strong.

> A: Which **industry** do you want to work in?
> B: The automobile **industry**, I think.

Introductory Exercises

A.   Match each word with its definition.

____	1. without a job	**a.** cooperate
____	2. certain	**b.** efficient
____	3. clear	**c.** expert
____	4. something used in a person's hand to do a job	**d.** industry
____	5. to stop	**e.** nowadays
____	6. with someone	**f.** obvious
____	7. the money paid for each hour of work	**g.** possible
____	8. able to work fast and well	**h.** quit
____	9. to educate for a job	**i.** similar
____	10. a person who does something very well	**j.** sure
____	11. to work together to do something	**k.** together
____	12. able to happen	**l.** tool
____	13. not the same, but not totally different	**m.** train
____	14. at this time	**n.** unemployed
		o. wage

B.   Answer each question with a word from the word form chart in this unit.

1. What can you do if you don't like your job?
2. If two people must work together, what should they do?
3. What do people use to build a house?
4. What do workers earn?
5. Who knows how to do something very well?
6. What do you call something that may happen?
7. What is someone who works very fast and well?
8. What is a person who does not have a job?

Study Exercises

C. Write **T** if the sentence is true and **F** if it is false.

_____ **1.** If something is impossible, it is easy to do.

_____ **2.** After you quit your job, you may be unemployed.

_____ **3.** Many workers use tools.

_____ **4.** An expert is not trained.

_____ **5.** Similar things are totally different.

_____ **6.** Factory workers often receive hourly wages.

_____ **7.** Employers want to hire efficient employees.

_____ **8.** When a person works alone, he must cooperate.

_____ **9.** There are no factories in an industrial area.

_____ **10.** It is not easy to see something that is obvious.

D. In the blanks, write the appropriate word(s) from the word form chart in this unit.

1. That factory produces many cars each day; it is very

_____ .

2. That _____ is very respected for his skill in his work.

3. That company _____-s its new employees for two
months.

4. Unfortunately, there are many _____ people who are
looking for work nowadays.

5. Because he hated his job, he _____ .

6. The members of a team must _____ .

7. We are attempting to find the answer to that problem, but

the answer is not _____ .

8. A salary is _____ to wages.

9. I am _____ about that information; I know it is true.

10. When I locked my keys in my car, the police used a

_____ to open the door.

E. Read the passage and answer the questions that follow.

Last year, John Smith and Sam Brown, the owners of the People Mover Bus Company, faced a different problem. After months of working on the problem, they were sure that no answer was possible, but as a last attempt, they decided to
5 hire an expert.

When the expert arrived, Mr. Smith and Mr. Brown explained the problem to him: in the past, their factory had been very efficient, producing more than fifteen buses each day. Nowadays the factory was producing only about ten
10 buses each day. Because the bus industry is very competitive, it was obvious that Mr. Smith and Mr. Brown were sure to lose money if no answer was found.

The expert had been trained to study factories and help them be more efficient. He had helped factory owners with
15 similar problems in the past. The expert talked to the workers about their work conditions. He found that their wages were high, and the tools that they used were excellent. But many of the workers had quit during the last year, so the number of new workers was very high. These new workers
20 needed training to know how to cooperate with the other workers.

The owners found that more training for the new workers was the answer to their efficiency problem.

1. Who did the owners decide to hire? _____

_____

2. What was the problem in the factory? _____

_____

3. What training had the expert had? _____

_____

4. Who had the expert helped in the past? _____

_____

5. Why did the factory have many new workers? _____

_____

6. What kind of training did the new workers need? _____

_____

Follow-up

F.   Dictation: Write the sentences that your teacher reads aloud.

1. _____

2. _____

3. _____

4. _____

5. _____

G.   Answer the following questions.

1. Which industries have the highest wages in your country? The lowest?
2. Which jobs require the most training? Why?
3. Do people in your country often quit their jobs?
4. Name some jobs that require tools.
5. Which parts of your country are the most industrialized?
6. Have you quit a job? Why?
7. Are you an expert at anything? What?
8. What can you do very efficiently?
9. In what ways do students in your country cooperate with each other?
10. Which languages are similar to your language? How are they similar?

H.   What kind of workers do employers like to hire? Explain.

Buying and Selling

Word Form Chart

NOUN	VERB	ADJECTIVE	ADVERB
deal	deal		
dealings			
dealer (人)			
guarantee	guarantee	guaranteed	
inferiority		inferior	
object			
			of course
origin	originate	original	originally
order	order		
percent			
percentage			
probability		probable	probably
improbability		improbable	improbably
quality			
reduction	reduce	reduced	
sale			
saving	save		
sign			

Definitions and Examples

1. **deal** (a) [a good bargain]

    She offered us a good **deal** on the furniture. We had to buy it.

    A: Did you get a good **deal** on your used car?
    B: No. I spent more than I wanted to.

    (b) [a promise to buy or sell something]

    We made a **deal** to sell our old car to a neighbor.

2. **guarantee** [a promise to return your money if there is a problem with the item you have bought]

    There is a **guarantee** on this television. It is **guaranteed** for 30 days.

    Clerk: This camera doesn't come with a **guarantee**.
    Customer: Then I don't want to buy it.

3. **object** [any thing that we can see; any item that we can think about]

    The **objects** on this table are expensive.

    A: Excuse me, miss. What's that **object** on the table?
    B: That's a lamp, sir.

4. **of course** [certainly]

    Of course, the purpose of the store is to make money.

    Customer: Do your cameras come with a guarantee?
    Clerk: **Of course**.

5. **order** [to ask for something; to ask that something be sent to you]*

    If the store does not have the camera you want, you can **order** it from the company.

    A: Here you are, sir. Your new color television.
    B: That's not what I **ordered**. I **ordered** a camera!

6. **original** [first or beginning]

    The **original** price was $78, but it went down to $60.

    A: Where's your new typewriter?
    B: I was going to buy one **originally**, but I decided to buy a television instead.

---

*For additional meanings of **order** see this Volume, Unit 11.

7. **percent** (%) [parts of a hundred]

   Fifty **percent** of their orders come from men, and the other half from women.

   A: The prices on color televisions are down by **30%**.
   B: I still don't want one.

8. **probably** [more than 50% certain]

   The company will **probably** guarantee its products.

   A: Are you going to buy a radio?
   B: Yes. I **probably** will.

9. **quality** [how good something is]

   People are interested in the **quality** of the products they buy.

   A: What do you look for in a new television?
   B: I look for price and **quality**.

10. **inferior** [of poor quality, especially in comparison to something else]

    These products are usually **inferior** to other, more expensive products.

    A: What do you think of your new television?
    B: I'm sorry that I bought it. It's **inferior** in quality.

11. **reduce** [to make smaller or lower]

    Prices are **reduced** by 50% this week because the stores wants to sell everything.

    A: They're asking for $450.
    B: Let's see if they'll **reduce** the price to $400.

12. **sale** [the selling of something, especially selling at a reduced price]

    Large stores have major **sales** once or twice a year.

    A: I'd like to buy it today, but it's too expensive.
    B: Wait until it goes on **sale**.

13. **save** (a) [to keep money or something else for the future; to avoid spending too much]

    Usually you **save** money when you pay in cash.

    A: Did you buy a used car?
    B: No. I haven't **saved** enough money yet.

    (b) [to take from danger]

    The child's father **saved** her from the fire.

14. **sign** [printed information that is placed where people can see it]
   The **sign** on the window said, "Sale today, 10% to 50% off."
   A: The door is still locked.
   B: The **sign** says the store opens today at 10 o'clock.

Introductory Exercises

A. Match each word with its definition.

_____ 1. bad or poor quality
_____ 2. to make something smaller
_____ 3. parts of a hundred
_____ 4. to keep your money
_____ 5. a promise to give your money back
_____ 6. the first or beginning
_____ 7. to ask that something be sent to you
_____ 8. anything we can see
_____ 9. more than 50% certain

a. deal
b. guarantee
c. inferior
d. object
e. of course
f. order
g. original
h. percent
i. probable
j. quality
k. reduce
l. sale
m. save
n. sign

B. Finish the sentence with a word from the word form chart in this unit.

1. The price of the camera is printed on this _____ .
2. A poor quality product is _____ .
3. Don't buy it today. Wait until it goes on _____ .
4. Tomorrow all prices will be reduced by 50 _____ .
5. Don't buy it without a _____ .
6. I don't like this new product. I prefer the _____ one.
7. I wasn't going to buy it, but she gave me a good _____ .
8. When they asked me if I wanted to buy it at half price, I said,
   " _____ ."
9. I won't take it unless you _____ the price.

Study Exercises

C.   Write **T** if the sentence is true and **F** if it is false.

      ____   **1.** Cheap products may be inferior.

      ____   **2.** A good deal is when you pay too much.

      ____   **3.** A reduced price always means reduced quality.

      ____   **4.** Guaranteed products are usually cheaper.

      ____   **5.** You can save money by not buying many things.

      ____   **6.** High quality things are usually expensive.

      ____   **7.** At a good sale, prices may be reduced by half.

      ____   **8.** Of course, the original price is higher than the sale price.

      ____   **9.** To make more money, dealers may increase the cost of something by a big percentage.

      ____   **10.** An object of inferior quality will probably last a very long time.

D.   Write sentences with the words.

1. is reduced / by 50% / the price

_____

2. not / this / for sale / object / is

_____

3. was / the / $5 / price / original

_____

4. you / the factory / order / this television / from / can

_____

5. the deal / I / a hundred dollars / saved / on

_____

6. the window / read / in / the sign / we

_____

7. all / the company / its products / guarantees

_____

E. Circle the word which is different.

1. probably   certainly   originally
2. quality   sign   value
3. first   inferior   original
4. on sale   reduced   guarantee
5. save   object   product
6. valuable   inferior   bad
7. buy   of course   order

F. Read the passage and answer the questions that follow.

    Everybody has to buy or sell things sometimes. Even students, who are usually not very rich, have to learn something about making purchases intelligently. As a student you may find, for example, that you need to buy a
5 typewriter or winter clothing. You may want to buy a television or a used car. Of course, you want to get good value for your money. If you are considering a major purchase, or any purchase, you should remember two important things.
10   1. Study first, and then decide what you want to buy. You can learn a lot just by reading books and advertisements.
    Remember that a high quality product will probably last longer and work better. Of course, for a superior product you can expect to pay more. An inferior product may not give
15 you the same quality, but the price should be low. Perhaps this seems obvious, but you must know the quality. Don't just look at the price. A poor quality product could be expensive. And a valuable one could be on sale at a greatly reduced price.
20   2. Don't hurry. Take your time. After you decide what product you want, go to many different stores. If you cannot find the product you want, you may try to order it directly from the factory. Or ask the store to order it for you.
    Look for a good deal. If you wait, you will probably find
25 that your product will go on sale and you may be able to save 10, 20, or even 50 percent off the original price.
    Finally, before you buy, make sure that the product is guaranteed. If you don't like it, you want to be able to get your money back.
30   If you carefully examine your own preferences and then shop until you find the lowest possible price, you will generally be happy with your purchase and also keep more money in the bank.

1. What are some things that students might purchase? _____

_____

2. Where can you get information about products? _____

_____

3. What is more important, quality or price? _____

_____

4. Why is it dangerous to judge a product by its price alone? _____

_____

5. If you know what you want, why wait? _____

_____

6. How much can you save if you wait for a sale? _____

_____

7. Why is a guarantee so important? _____

_____

Follow-up

G. Dictation: Write the sentences that your teacher reads aloud.

1. _____

2. _____

3. _____

4. _____

5. _____

H. Answer the following questions about your country.

1. What do students buy?
2. How do you find the best product for the lowest price?
3. Are there special prices for students? Where?

4. What products are very expensive? Very cheap?
5. Do you order products by mail? How long does it take?
6. Can you get your money back on a product if you're not satisfied?
7. When do stores have sales? How much are the products reduced?
8. Which products come with guarantees?
9. What objects do you value highly? Why?

I.   Tell a story about the following situation. What will happen?

      John decides one morning that he wants a color television. So, he gets on a bus and goes to a large store downtown.

Vacation

Word Form Chart

NOUN	VERB	ADJECTIVE	ADVERB
			abroad
adaptation	adapt	adaptable	
		adaptive	adaptively
		adapted	
		ancient	
approximation	approximate	approximate	approximately
arrangement	arrange	arranged	
			at least
calendar			
culture	acculturate	cultural	culturally
face	face		
hesitation	hesitate	hesitant	hesitantly
imitation	imitate	imitative	
loneliness		lonely	
museum			
		previous	previously
relaxation	relax	relaxed	
		relaxing	

Definitions and Examples

1. **abroad** [out of the country]

   I like to travel **abroad**. I always learn a lot while visiting other countries.

   A: I hear you take many trips **abroad**.
   B: Yes. My company does business in many countries, so I travel **abroad** often.

2. **calendar** [schedule of days, months]

   Is your **calendar** empty? If so, you must not be very busy.

   A: Can you go to lunch with Bob and me next week?
   B: I'll look at my **calendar** to be sure.

3. **face** (a) [to turn the front of the body to something]

   Students **face** the teachers in the classroom.
   Seats on a bus usually **face** the front.

   (b) [to accept something, usually a fact]

   When you travel abroad, you must **face** the fact that the country is very different from your own.

   A: **Face** it, your grades aren't very good this year.
   B: I know. I'll try to do better next year.

4. **culture** [different ways of doing things in different countries or in different groups of people, for example: clothes, food, holidays]

   Each country has a different **culture**. That's why it is so exciting to travel abroad.

   A: Did you enjoy the **culture** of the countries you visited?
   B: Yes, but I'm glad to be back in my own **culture** again!

5. **ancient** [very, very old]

   I like visiting Greece because there are so many **ancient** buildings to see.

   A: Are you interested in **ancient** cultures?
   B: No. I like modern things better.

6. **relax** [to rest after effort; to be comfortable; to do something you enjoy]

   Relaxing vacations are those which do not have busy schedules.

   A: I came to London to **relax**, but there are too many things to do!
   B: If you want to **relax**, go to the beach, not to a city!

7. **previous** [coming before a time or a thing]

   Stop! We've passed the street! The **previous** one was the right one.
   My **previous** trips abroad have been to Europe. This time I went to
   Africa.

8. **lonely** [to feel sad because of being alone]

   When I travel alone, I'm not usually **lonely** because I frequently
   meet new people.

   A: Isn't it **lonely** to be in Cairo without any friends or family?
   B: No. I like being alone.

9. **imitate** [to try to be like others]

   "When in Rome, do as the Romans do" means you should **imitate**
   the culture you are visiting.

   A: I bought a lot of clothes in Japan. I want to **imitate** the Japanese
   type of dress.
   B: You look very Japanese!

10. **adapt** (to) [to change something or someone to fit a new condition; to
    become comfortable with something]

    I didn't like living in Sweden. I couldn't **adapt to** the life there.

    A: How long did it take you to **adapt to** your new home?
    B: Not very long. I got to know the culture and the language very
    soon.

11. **museum** [a place to see ancient pictures, clothes, tools, and animals]

    Do you like art **museums** or history **museums**?

    A: We should visit the famous **museums** while we're in Paris.
    B: I prefer to walk around the city.

12. **approximate** [not exact; almost right]

    If you are not sure of something, you give an **approximate** answer.

    A: How far is it to the museum from here?
    B: I'm not sure, but I think it's **approximately** one mile.

13. **arrangement** [a plan]

    It is sometimes difficult to make **arrangements** to stay in a hotel
    before you go abroad.

    A: I **arranged** everything for our trip.
    B: Good. Now we can leave for our vacation with no worries!

14. **hesitate** [to wait a little; to wait before deciding something because of not being sure]

> Don't **hesitate**. If you buy your plane tickets now, they'll be cheaper!
>
> A: Do you have any **hesitations** about going abroad?
> B: Yes. I'm not sure I can adapt to the culture very well.

15. **at least** [not less than]

> Our plane tickets will cost **at least** $1,000, probably more.
>
> A: What time is it?
> B: I don't know, but it's **at least** 5:00. We've been walking for hours since lunch.

Introductory Exercises

A. Match each word with its definition.

_____ 1. out of the country

_____ 2. very, very old

_____ 3. sad about being alone

_____ 4. schedule of days, months

_____ 5. almost correct

_____ 6. before

_____ 7. a plan

_____ 8. not less than

a. abroad
b. adapt
c. ancient
d. approximate
e. arrangement
f. at least
g. calendar
h. culture
i. lonely
j. previous

B. Say the appropriate word from the word form chart.

1. When Hugo travels, he likes to _____ everything early. He likes to plan early.

2. Do you feel some _____ about going abroad alone? Are you afraid?

3. My mother likes to visit _____-s on our vacations.

4. I don't want to make too many plans. On my vacation, I want to _____ .

5. The fun of traveling abroad is learning all about a new

_____ .

6. Tom likes to visit places with _____ buildings and roads.

7. It's fun to try to _____ the speakers of a new language when you travel; you can try to speak like them.

8. When Tanya went to Turkey, it took her a long time to _____ to the new culture.

Study Exercises

C. Write **T** if the sentence is true and **F** if it is false.

____ 1. If you really want to go somewhere, you are very hesitant.

____ 2. When you are not sure of the time, you can give an approximate answer.

____ 3. When you travel inside your country, you are traveling abroad.

____ 4. It is very easy to imitate new customs and languages when you are in a new country.

____ 5. If Sue needs at least two more courses to finish school, she cannot graduate after taking only one.

____ 6. To face your problems is often difficult and unpleasant.

____ 7. When you are with your friends at home you are usually lonely.

____ 8. It is possible to arrange your vacation after you take it.

____ 9. Museums are big, open places where you can have a picnic.

____ 10. Calendars usually show twelve months.

D. Fill in the blanks with word(s) from the word form chart in this unit.

1. When Jerry moved to Australia, he found it very difficult to _____ to his new life.

2. Jerry was _____ because he had no friends.

3. It was difficult to meet anyone because Jerry was _____ to talk to new people.

4. Jerry tried to _____ the way that Australians talked, but he did not sound the same.

5. Finally, Jerry met some people who had moved to Australia two years _____ . They knew the problems of living abroad.

6. His new friends helped him learn how to _____ the difficulties of the new culture.

7. With his new friends Jerry began to _____ and enjoy Australia.

E. Read the passage and answer the questions that follow.

When you go abroad, there are a number of things to remember to have a successful trip. There are at least three important areas of every new culture you must adapt to: the language, the food, and the clothing. The best thing to do is
5 to try to imitate the people of the country. If they speak French, don't try to communicate in Chinese! If they eat fish for breakfast, don't hesitate! You too can try fish for breakfast. If you know they go shopping in fancy clothes, arrange to take some nice clothes with you before you go.
10   Your vacation can be relaxing and pleasant if you follow these ideas. If you have never traveled abroad previously, it may be difficult to face the problems you meet. But don't worry! You can always get away from cultural difficulties by visiting some ancient buildings or museums. Look at your
15 calendar to be sure you have approximately two to three hours free every day for these relaxing visits. But don't spend all your time alone or you will be lonely. Arrange to spend some time every day making friends. In this way you can learn about the new culture, and have fun, too!

1. What three areas must you adapt to in a new culture?

    a. _____

    b. _____

    c. _____

2. What should you do if the people eat fish for breakfast? _____

_____

3. How will your vacation be if you follow the ideas in the passage? ____

_____

4. How can you get away from cultural problems for a short time? ____

_____

5. How much time should you leave free every day for relaxing visits to museums or ancient buildings? _____

_____

Follow-up

F. Dictation: Write the sentences that your teacher reads aloud.

1. _____

2. _____

3. _____

4. _____

5. _____

G. Answer the following questions.

1. Have you every traveled abroad? Where?
2. Have you ever made your own arrangements for a trip? How?
3. Do you like museums? What kinds?
4. Are you ever lonely? When?
5. Do you prefer ancient or modern buildings?
6. Have you ever had to face something difficult? What?
7. Which sounds in English are difficult for you to imitate?
8. Name one part of your culture that is different from American or British culture.
9. Have you ever had to adapt to a new place? When?
10. What is the most relaxing vacation you have taken?
11. Is it easy to make friends in a new culture?

H. Describe a trip abroad that you or someone you know has taken.

Recreation/Entertainment

Word Form Chart

NOUN	VERB	ADJECTIVE	ADVERB
act			
actor ⚥	act	acting	
actress ⚥			
amusement	amuse	amused	
		amusing	amusingly
ballet			
ballerina ⚥			
cancellation	cancel	cancelled	
circle	circle	circled	
		circling	
	encircle		
		circular	
climax	climax	climactic	
diameter			diametrically
drama	dramatize	dramatic	dramatically
dramatist ⚥			
dramatization			
entertainment	entertain	entertained	
entertainer ⚥		entertaining	entertainingly
form	form	formed	
		imaginary	
imagination	imagine	imaginative	imaginatively
performance	perform	performed	
		performing	
performer ⚥			
sound	sound		
stare	stare	staring	
theater		theatrical	theatrically
variety	vary	various	variously
variation		varied	

Definitions and Examples

1. **act** [to play the part of a person in a movie or a play]

    My uncle **acts** in movies. He usually plays the part of a policeman.

    A: Who is the **actor** who played Kojak?
    B: His name is Telly Savalas.

2. **amuse** [to make people smile, laugh, or enjoy themselves]

    My sister's children **amuse** me very much. They always do funny things.

    A: Did you like the movie last night?
    B: Yes. I thought it was very **amusing**.

3. **ballet** [a kind of dance with formal jumps and moves, usually telling a story]

    A **ballet** dancer must train for many years.
    One of the most famous **ballet** groups in the world is the Bolshoi **Ballet** in Moscow. There are also many famous Russian **ballet** dancers like Rudolf Nureyev and Mikhail Baryshnikov.

    A: Do you go to the **ballet** often?
    B: Only sometimes; I prefer modern dance.

4. **cancel** [to put an end to something before it starts]

    We **cancelled** our vacation in California because my husband broke his leg.

    A: I bought a ticket for the ballet tonight, but now I can't go.
    B: You should **cancel** your tickets.
    A: I can't—the theater doesn't accept **cancellations**. Do you want my ticket?
    B: Sure. I'd love to see the ballet.

5. **form** (a) [the way something looks]

    I made a cake in the **form** of the letter "T."

    (b) [a way of doing something]

    Last night I saw a group that performs an ancient **form** of dancing.

    (c) [to make in a certain way]

    The students **formed** a group to study for the test.

6. **circle** [something that has the form of the letter "O"]

   The students sit in a **circle** in the classroom.
   The houses in my neighborhood are built in a **circle** around a small park.

   Teacher: On this test you must **circle** the mistake in the sentence.
   Student: Should we write the correct sentence?
   Teacher: No. Only **circle** the part of the sentence that's wrong.

7. **diameter** [the distance across a circle]

   The **diameter** of a golf ball is smaller than the **diameter** of a basketball.
   The child made a circle with a **diameter** of one meter in the sand.

8. **climax** [the most exciting part of a play or story]

   The **climax** of the play was when the man tried to murder his wife.

   A: What did you think of the movie?
   B: I thought the first part was boring, but the **climax** was very good.

9. **drama** (a) [the study of writing and acting plays]

   A person who studies **drama** learns how to make plays for an audience.

   (b) [a play]

   A: Did you watch TV last night?
   B: Yes. I saw a Shakespearean **drama**.

   A **dramatist** is a person who writes plays.

10. **perform** [to do something, for example, to sing, dance, act, or play music—in front of a group of people]

    The musician **performed** several piano pieces by Beethoven at the concert last night.

    A: At what time are the students going to **perform** the play?
    B: I think the **performance** begins at 8:00.

11. **entertain** [to amuse people with a performance]

    The young man **entertained** the audience by playing the guitar and singing.
    The soldiers were **entertained** by the actor's jokes.

    A: What did you do this weekend?
    B: I went to the ballet. It was very enjoyable and **entertaining**.

12. **imagine** [to see a picture in your thoughts]

When we are afraid, we **imagine** things that are not true.
Can you **imagine** a world without wars and fighting?
An author needs a lot of **imagination** to write good mystery stories.

13. **stare** [to look hard for a long time at something or someone]

When you **stare** at something, you look at it for a long time.
The child **stared** at the 1920 car. He had never seen an old car like
    that before.

Mother: Don't **stare** at the lady. It's not nice.
Daughter: I'm not **staring** at her. I'm trying to read her newspaper.

14. **theater** [a place where plays are performed by actors in front of an
audience]

People go to a **theater** to see plays and sometimes concerts and
    ballets.
I had a ticket to go to the **theater** last night, but I had to cancel it
    because I got sick.

A: What did you do last night?
B: We went to the **theater** to see a play by Arthur Miller, an
    American dramatist.

15. **sound** [anything you can hear]

The **sound** of the train behind my house always wakes me up.
The **sound** of the ocean is very restful.

A: I don't like to go to that theater.
B: Why not?
A: The **sound** is bad. You can't easily hear any of the actors' words.

16. **various** [different; several]

Big cities have **various** types of entertainment: movies, plays,
    dance, concerts.
There are **various** ways to travel from New York to California; you
    can fly, take a train, or drive. The cost of each method **varies**.
    Flying is the most expensive.

Introductory Exercises

A. Match each word with its definition.

____	1. to see a picture in your thoughts	**a.**	actor
____	2. a place where plays are acted	**b.**	amuse
____	3. the most exciting part of a play	**c.**	cancel
____	4. to look at something for a long time	**d.**	climax
____	5. to make people smile or laugh	**e.**	diameter
____	6. anything you hear	**f.**	drama
____	7. a play	**g.**	entertain
____	8. a person who plays a part in a movie or play	**h.**	form
____	9. several, different	**i.**	imagine
____	10. to do something in front of an audience	**j.**	perform
____	11. the distance across a circle	**k.**	sound
		l.	stare
		m.	theater
		n.	various

B. Answer each question with a word from the word form chart in this unit.

1. Where do you go to see a play?
2. What do you call a woman who acts?
3. If someone is looking at you for a long time, what is he doing?
4. What is the most exciting part of a play?
5. If you order a ticket and then decide not to use it, what should you do to the ticket?
6. If a movie makes you laugh, what does it do to you?
7. What is the form of a ring?
8. What does an actor do in the theater?
9. What can you measure to find the size of a circle?

Study Exercises

C. Write **T** if the sentence is true and **F** if it is false.

____ 1. People often cry at amusing movies.

____ 2. Americans think it is nice to stare at other people.

____ 3. A good ballet dancer must train for many years.

___ **4.** An author needs a good imagination.

___ **5.** The symbol for the Olympics is formed with two circles.

___ **6.** A dramatist is a person who acts in movies.

___ **7.** Basketball games are a form of entertainment.

___ **8.** The diameter of a circle may be big or small.

___ **9.** The climax of a play is the most boring part.

___ **10.** Dramas are usually performed in theaters.

___ **11.** If a play is cancelled, you should arrive early to see it.

D. In the blanks, write the appropriate word(s) from the word form chart.

1. If you describe your family, I can _____ what they look like.

2. The supermarket near my house has good vegetables, but it does not have much _____ . Usually there are only a few kinds.

3. We saw a movie last night, but I didn't understand it. The picture was clear, but the _____ wasn't very good.

4. I always cry if someone dies in a _____ performance.

5. I don't like modern dance, but I love _____ .

6. There are usually two times to see a play in one day: there is a _____ at 2:00 in the afternoon and another one at 8:00 in the evening.

7. A dinner theater has food and _____ ; first, you eat dinner; then you see a play.

8. The hotel swimming pool is in the _____ of the letter "L."

9. Small children often _____ at unusual people.

10. My aunt is a famous _____ . She has been in many plays.

E. Read the passage and answer the questions that follow.

Anne is from Akron, Ohio. Her dream has always been
to visit London, England. She imagined London as a big,
exciting city with some of the best drama in the world. This
summer her dream came true when she spent a week in
5 London. She stayed in a hotel in the theater area, and on the
first day she took several long walks through the city, staring
at all the famous buildings. Because there is a wide variety of
entertainment in London, she could go to a different theater
every night. The first night she saw a comedy by Tom
10 Stoppard, which was very amusing. The second night she
went to a performance of <u>Swan Lake</u> by the Royal Ballet,
because <u>Swan Lake</u> is her favorite ballet. But the climax of
her trip was when she went to see a play by the most famous
dramatist in the English language—Shakespeare. She saw a
15 performance of <u>King Lear</u> at the Old Vic Theater with one of
the best English actors, Laurence Olivier. Anne had never
imagined that she would see a play by Shakespeare performed
in London! This was her most enjoyable vacation.

1. What has always been Anne's dream? _____

_____

2. Where did she stay in London? _____

_____

3. What did she do the first day? _____

_____

4. What did she see the first night? _____

_____

5. What did she see the second night? _____

_____

6. What was the climax of the trip? _____

_____

Follow-up

F. Dictation: Write the sentences that your teacher reads aloud.

1. _____

2. _____

3. _____

4. _____

5. _____

G. Answer the following questions.

1. What is your favorite form of entertainment?
2. Describe your favorite drama in your language.
3. What sound does a cat make in your language? a dog? a chicken?
4. Describe various ways you can meet people when you live in a foreign country.
5. Describe an amusing movie you have seen.
6. Name several things you can cancel.
7. Who are the best actor and actress in your country?
8. Name several things that are like a circle.
9. What did you imagine this school was like before you came here?

H. Tell a story about the following situation. What will happen?

You are in your country. A student from another country is going to live with your family for a month. What kinds of entertainment do you want the student to see?

Science

Word Form Chart

NOUN	VERB	ADJECTIVE	ADVERB
astronomy		astronomical	astronomically
astronomer ⚲			
collection	collect	collected	
collector ⚲		collective	collectively
complexity		complex	
curiosity		curious	curiously
data			
determination	determine	determined	determinedly
drop	drop	dropped	
		dropping	
experiment	experiment	experimental	experimentally
figure	figure		
gravity	gravitate	gravitational	
logic		logical	logically
		illogical	illogically
physics			
physicist ⚲			
power	power	powerful	powerfully
		powerless	powerlessly
secret		secret	secretly
		secretive	secretively
system	systematize	systematic	systematically

Definitions and Examples

1. **figure** (a) [a number]

    A mathematician works with **figures**.

    A: Did you prepare those **figures** for the cost of the program?
    B: I'll finish them this afternoon.

    (b) [to find an answer, usually using numbers]

    To **figure** the cost of going to the university, you should add the
     price of tuition, books, and transportation.

2. **physics** [the scientific study of the laws that control light, movement,
    sound, heat, and electricity]

    Most engineers study a lot of **physics**.
    Albert Einstein was a famous **physicist**.

    A: Are you going to take a **physics** class in the fall?
    B: No, because I need to study more math first.

3. **complex** [having many parts; difficult to understand]

    An airplane is a **complex** machine.
    Physics is a **complex** subject.
    The **complexity** of this problem makes it difficult to find the
     answer.

4. **astronomy** [the scientific study of the moon, sun, and other objects in
    the sky]

    In **astronomy** classes, students use complex instruments to study
     the sky.
    Copernicus was the **astronomer** who discovered that the Earth
     circles the sun.

5. **determine** [to find an answer or explanation]

    Using complex tools, the astronomers were able to **determine** the
     exact temperature of three areas of the moon.
    Scientists have **determined** the approximate age of many ancient
     buildings.

6. **experiment** [a scientific test to investigate or discover something]

> Children do **experiments** with plants in biology class. For example, they may put the plant in a dark place to see if it grows.
> Some **experiments** require complex machines.
>
> A: What method does your English teacher use?
> B: It's an **experimental** one.
> A: What do you mean?
> B: The method is new. The teacher is trying it to see if it works.

7. **collect** [to bring together in one place]

> When I was a child, I **collected** stamps from many countries. My **collection** had more than 1,500 stamps.
>
> A: Do you have any hobbies?
> B: Yes. I'm a book **collector**. I own many valuable books.

8. **data** {requires plural verb} [facts, usually in the form of numbers]

> Astronomers watch the moon to get **data** about its movements.
> Once every ten years, the United States government collects **data** about the number of people in every city.
>
> A: Do you believe the explanation in this article?
> B: No. The **data** aren't complete, and I don't think they're correct.

9. **secret** [information that you do not want others to know]

> Military plans must be **secret**. If many people know about the plans, the enemy may discover them.
> My sister is a very **secretive** person. She acts mysteriously and will not tell us what she is thinking.
>
> Child A: I know a **secret**, and I won't tell you.
> Child B: Please!
> Child A: No. I promised that I wouldn't tell.

10. **system** [an exact and orderly method of doing something; an exact arrangement of something]

> The body has one **system** for using air and another one for using food.
> Astronomers study **systems** of objects in the sky.
> Scientists must be very **systematic**. They must do each part of their work at the correct time and with an exact method.

11. **logical** [according to a clear and systematic way of thinking]

   Scientists try to find **logical** explanations for surprising facts.
   In **logic** classes, students learn about exact methods of thinking.

   Policeman A: Do you think that my explanation of the crime is
                    correct?
   Policeman B: No. It isn't **logical**. You say that the murder was
                    because of money, but the murderer is very rich. He
                    doesn't need money.

12. **curious** [very interested in learning and knowing things]

   If you are **curious** about French culture, you should go to France.
   Cats are very **curious** animals. Their **curiosity** is sometimes
       dangerous for them: they explore dark and dangerous places.

13. **drop** (a) [to allow something to fall]

   If you **drop** a glass, it will break.
   Planes **drop** bombs during a war.

   (b) [to go down]

   Prices **drop** if there is a big supply of a product.
   The temperature **dropped** during the night, from 40° F to 30° F.

14. **power** [official control; ability to do something; strength]

   The leaders of the United States and the Soviet Union are very
       powerful men.
   The head of a company has the **power** to hire employees and decide
       their salaries.
   Jack has **powerful** arms. He can lift heavy boxes.

   A: Do you think this engine has enough **power**?
   B: Yes. It has enough to push those old cars a few miles.

15. **gravity** [the power that holds people and objects on the earth]

   According to some stories, Isaac Newton discovered **gravity** when
       an apple fell on his head.
   Physicists study the laws of **gravity**.
   The **gravitational** pull of the moon changes the level of the waves
       on the beach.

Introductory Exercises

A. Match each word with its definition.

_____ 1. the science of objects in the sky

_____ 2. a number

_____ 3. very interested in knowing things

_____ 4. to allow something to fall

_____ 5. a scientific test

_____ 6. strength or official control

_____ 7. information that only a few people know

_____ 8. the science of laws about light, movement, etc.

_____ 9. to bring together in one place

_____ 10. an exact and orderly method of doing something

_____ 11. to find an answer

_____ 12. difficult to understand

a. astronomy
b. collect
c. complex
d. curious
e. determine
f. drop
g. experiment
h. figure
i. gravity
j. logical
k. physics
l. power
m. secret
n. system

B. Answer each question with a word from the word form chart in this unit.

1. What power holds people on the earth?
2. Which scientists study the moon?
3. Which scientists study light and sound?
4. What do scientists do to get information?
5. What are the figures that show the results of an experiment?
6. What kind of people ask many questions?
7. What kind of explanation is very clear and systematic?
8. What information is very private?
9. What happens if you hold something carelessly?
10. What can you do if you want many stamps?

Study Exercises

C. Write **T** if the sentence is true and **F** if it is false.

——— **1.** Lazy people are usually curious.

——— **2.** The lives of famous actors are usually secret.

——— **3.** The method of an experiment must be logical.

——— **4.** Astronomers try to locate systems in the sky.

——— **5.** A stamp collector probably does not have many stamps.

——— **6.** Gravity makes objects jump.

——— **7.** Some physics professors study gravity.

——— **8.** Scientists should collect data systematically.

——— **9.** It is difficult to determine the diameter of a circle.

——— **10.** If you drop a glass, it will probably break.

——— **11.** To study physics you need a theater.

——— **12.** To imagine a beautiful house, you need complex tools.

D. In the blanks, write the appropriate word(s) from the word form chart in this unit.

1. In chemistry class one method of learning is to do an

———————— .

2. Scientists must have a careful ——————— of collecting data.

3. A ——————— teacher might do experiments about gravity.

4. A thermometer is a thing that ———————-s the temperature.

5. Children often ask, "Why?" They are very ——————— .

6. I do not understand how this machine works. It's too

———————— .

7. The government published no data about the physicists' discovery.

8. It was a ——————— .

9. My watch broke when I ———————-ed it.

10. People study ——————— because they are curious about objects in the sky.

11. I have to do this experiment again because I did not get

enough ——————— the first time.

12. The astronomy book is easy to understand. The writing is very

———————— .

13. The university is _____-ing money to build a new science building.

E. Circle the word which is different.

1. figure   number   secret
2. interested   curious   boring
3. difficult   complex   clear
4. calendar   facts   data
5. physics   democracy   chemistry
6. fall   destroy   drop

F. Read the passage and answer the questions that follow.

Igor X is a physicist who studies topics related to gravity. He works for the government of his country, doing secret experiments in a secret building in the capital city. Everything is secret because the government is afraid that its
5   enemies will steal Igor's data and use the information to get more power.

Igor, like any good scientist, works very systematically. He plans each experiment carefully and writes the data in clear figures to avoid errors. He does each experiment several
10   times to be sure that the data are always the same. When he has collected a lot of data, he tries to think of a logical explanation for them.

Igor's curiosity has led him to some exciting discoveries. In 1986 he was working with a team of scientists who
15   discovered a power related to gravity. When the scientists tried to determine why an object moved in a certain way, they found that gravity could not explain everything. This discovery did not make Igor famous, but it was the climax of his studies.

1. What is Igor X's job? _____

_____

2. What are his experiments on? _____

_____

3. Why is his work secret? _____

_____

4. Write some facts about Igor's work method. _____

_____

5. What is the result of Igor's curiosity? _____

_____

6. What did Igor discover in 1986? _____

_____

Follow-up

G. Dictation: Write the sentences that your teacher reads aloud.

1. _____

2. _____

3. _____

4. _____

5. _____

H. Answer the following questions.

1. Have you ever done an experiment? About what?
2. Have you ever collected anything? What?
3. Tell me something that you should do systematically.
4. Tell me something which, in your opinion, is illogical.
5. Write a figure on the blackboard.
6. Does the temperature ever drop to less than 32° F in your city? During which month(s)?
7. Who has the most power in your country?
8. In your opinion, should scientific discoveries be available internationally, or should they be secret? What kind of data should be secret?
9. What countries are you curious about?
10. What interests you most about astronomy?

I. Tell a story about the following situation. What will happen?

Catherine Goodwin studied physics and astronomy at the university. She has just received an advanced degree, and she will begin working for a large company. Tell about her work.

Housing (B)

Word Form Chart

NOUN	VERB	ADJECTIVE	ADVERB
avenue			
cabin			
closet			
complaint	complain	complaining	complainingly
complainer ⚥			
construction	construct	constructed	
hall			
ideal		ideal	ideally
manager ⚥	manage	managing	
		managerial	managerially
management			
repair	repair	repaired	
residence	reside	residential	
resident ⚥			
roof			
shelf	shelve		
signature	sign	signed	
sink			
stairs			upstairs
			downstairs

Definitions and Examples

1. **manager** [a person who directs an office or a business]

   Most large apartment buildings have a **manager**.

   A: We'd like to have a look at the apartment upstairs.
   B: You'll have to talk to the **manager**.

2. **avenue** [a street, often a large street]

   The building is on Park **Avenue**.

   A: What's your address?
   B: 4831 Fifth **Ave**.

3. **cabin** [a very small house]

   They spend summers at a **cabin** in the mountains.

   A: They're rich. They have a summer home.
   B: Well, it's just a **cabin** near the ocean.

4. **closet** [a very small room where you store clothing]

   The bedroom has two large **closets**.

   A: Your rooms are really small.
   B: It's like living in a **closet**.

5. **complain** [to say that you are not satisfied with something]

   The guests **complained** about the small room.

   A: My apartment is too cold.
   B: **Complain** to the landlord.

6. **ideal** [perfect; what you like best]

   An **ideal** location for a home would be near a park.
   Ideally, a house should have a lot of storage space.

   A: What are you looking for?
   B: A small apartment near the university would be **ideal** for me.

7. **construct** [to build]

   The house was **constructed** 25 years ago.

   A: This building cost only $100,000 twenty years ago.
   B: Sure. **Construction** costs were lower then.

8. **hall** [an area to walk through inside a house or building]

   The bathroom is at the end of the **hall**.

   A: Where's the landlady?
   B: She just went down the **hall**.

9. **repair** [to put right something that is broken]

   The manager hired someone to **repair** the floor.

   A: The air conditioner isn't working right.
   B: Let's get somebody to **repair** it.

10. **sink** [a place in the kitchen or bathroom where you put water for washing]

    The kitchen **sink** leaks, but the manager will repair it.

    A: What did you do with my cup?
    B: It's in the **sink**.

11. **residence** [a home]

    The people who **reside** in this building are mostly office workers.

    A: Is this address your office or your **residence**?
    B: My **residence**.

12. **roof** [the top of a house or building]

    The **roof** was repaired last summer.

    A: What's wrong with the **roof**?
    B: It leaks.

13. **shelf** {plural: **shelves**}

    Students often make their own book **shelves**.

    A: Put the book back on the **shelf**, would you?
    B: Which **shelf**?

14. **sign** [to write your name]

    Have a lawyer read the lease before you **sign** it.

    A: Where do I **sign**?
    B: Right there. Write your usual signature.

15. **stairs**

    The **stairs** are made of expensive hardwood.
    There are two bedrooms **upstairs**.

Introductory Exercises

A. Match each word with its definition.

____	1. a very small house	**a.**	avenue
____	2. the top of a house	**b.**	cabin
____	3. to build	**c.**	closet
____	4. a home	**d.**	complain
____	5. a very small room where you store clothing	**e.**	construct
		f.	hall
____	6. to put right something that is broken	**g.**	ideal
		h.	manager
____	7. to write your name	**i.**	repair
____	8. perfect; what you like best	**j.**	residence
____	9. to say that you are not satisfied with something	**k.**	roof
		l.	shelf
____	10. an area to walk through inside a home or building	**m.**	sign
		n.	sink
		o.	stairs

B. Answer each question with a word from the word form chart in this unit.

1. What do people do when they're not satisfied with something?
2. What do you call the place where someone lives?
3. Where do you put dirty cups and plates?
4. Where do you put books?
5. What do people often do if something is broken?
6. Where do you put your clothes?
7. What's another name for a street?
8. What do you walk up or down in a house?
9. What do people call something that is perfect?
10. Who is the person who directs an office or a business?

Study Exercises

C. Write **T** if the sentence is true and **F** if it is false.

____ 1. Most people live in cabins.

____ 2. Your residence is where you live.

____ 3. The roof is in the basement of a house.

____ 4. You may find cabins in the mountains or near a beach.

____ 5. Most apartments do not have sinks.

____ 6. The manager of an apartment building may not be the owner.

____ 7. Bedrooms usually have closets.

____ 8. All houses have stairs.

____ 9. Avenues are found mainly on farms.

____ 10. Old buildings often need a lot of repairs.

D. In the blanks, write the appropriate word(s) from the word form chart in this unit.

1. If the hot water is not working in your apartment, you might call the _____ .

2. A small, inexpensive apartment near the university would be _____ for a student.

3. Clothes can be hung up in the _____ .

4. If the air conditioner does not work, you should call someone to _____ it.

5. When she was tired of reading, she put the book back on the _____ .

6. The dirty glasses are all in the _____ .

7. For their vacation they went to the mountains, where they stayed in a _____ .

8. To repair the leak you will have to climb up on the _____ .

9. The manager lives _____ , not upstairs.

10. The building is located on Fifth _____ .

E. Circle the word which is different.

1. street   park   avenue

2. bathroom   bedroom   cabin

3. repair   break   destroy

4. preferable   perfect   ideal

5. reside   live   work

6. roof   top   basement

7. office   residence   house

8. sink   shelf   complaint

9. closet   manager   hall

F.   Read the passage and answer the questions that follow.

Many American undergraduates live in dormitories during the first year of college or university. But after the first year of study, many of these students prefer to rent housing of their own. Many graduate students and
5 international students also look for apartments or houses to rent near the university where they are studying.

Although students like the greater freedom and comfort that they can find off campus, they may sometimes be disappointed with their housing. If you are looking for an
10 apartment or house to rent, look carefully and think carefully before you sign a lease. A typical lease is for one year, so if you do not like your new housing, you may be unhappy in it for a long time before you can move to a better place.

While you look, ask yourself some questions. Does the
15 house or apartment have what you need? Is it large enough? Find out if there are enough closets and room for storage. How is the location? Probably you want a place that is convenient to stores, transportation, and your school. Does it have enough furniture, or will you have to buy some more?
20 Most apartments have a stove and refrigerator, but make sure.

Is the apartment quiet? You may have noisy neighbors upstairs, downstairs, or on either side of you. If you have a car, ask if there is a garage or other space for parking. Find
25 out, too, what you should do if something goes wrong in your apartment. The manager may live in the building, or the landlord may have special telephone numbers for you to call if, for example, the roof leaks or if you are having a problem with the sink.
30 Most students do not have much time or money to spend on the search for good housing. Probably you will not be lucky enough to find an ideal place to live. But if you look carefully and ask yourself the right questions, you will make a better decision. A comfortable and convenient apartment
35 can make your university experience much more enjoyable.

1. Where do students live in the United States? _____

_____

2. How long is the typical lease? _____

_____

3. What questions should you ask yourself about the following, before renting your apartment?

a) its size _____

b) its location _____

c) furniture/kitchen items _____

d) noise _____

e) parking _____

f) repairs _____

Follow-up

G. Dictation: Write the sentences that your teacher reads aloud.

1. _____

2. _____

3. _____

4. _____

5. _____

H. Answer the following questions.

1. Where do students live in your country?
2. Describe a typical dormitory.
3. Is student housing expensive?
4. Is housing difficult to find?
5. Do students have many problems with landlords and landladies?
6. Who does repairs in rented housing?
7. Are there problems with heating and cooling?
8. What kind of housing would be ideal for you?

I. Tell a story about the following situation. What will happen?

The new school year begins next week. John still doesn't have a place to live. Yesterday, walking by a large apartment building, he saw a "For Rent" sign. He rang the bell of the manager's office.

Answer Key

Unit 1

C. **1.** T **2.** T **3.** F **4.** T **5.** T **6.** T **7.** F **8.** F **9.** F **10.** T

D. **1.** educated **2.** pass **3.** compulsory **4.** error **5.** private **6.** level **7.** advanced **8.** absent/missing **9.** examples **10.** type **11.** public

E. **I.** **1.** f **2.** c **3.** g **4.** h **5.** b
II. **1.** f **2.** e **3.** b **4.** d

F. **1.** sixteen **2.** seventeen or eighteen **3.** almost half **4.** no **5.** find jobs

Unit 2

C. **1.** F **2.** T **3.** F **4.** F **5.** T **6.** T **7.** F **8.** T **9.** T **10.** T **11.** T

D. **1.** more **2.** a lot of **3.** will **4.** will not **5.** annually **6.** high **7.** excellent

E. **1.** proud **2.** produce **3.** hire **4.** owns **5.** salary **6.** until **7.** conditions **8.** annual **9.** part-time **10.** lazy **11.** monthly **12.** expect **13.** less **14.** excellent **15.** effort

F. **1.** at the campus travel company **2.** when he was a student **3.** excellent working conditions and advantages because he works at the university **4.** wants to work for a bigger company **5.** excellent skills and a lot of work **6.** no **7.** once a month **8.** three weeks **9.** yes **10.** (student's opinion)

Unit 3

C. **1.** location **2.** block **3.** satisfied, size **4.** pick **5.** area **6.** improved **7.** available **8.** convenient

D. **1.** satisfaction **2.** available **3.** for sale **4.** pick

E. 1. The schedule of the language lab is inconvenient.   2. These gloves are not my size.   3. Wooden barns are often painted red in the United States. 4. The child picked blue curtains for her room.   5. My improvement did not satisfy the teacher.   6. Information on this town is available at the library.

F. 1. F 2. T 3. F 4. T 5. F 6. T 7. T 8. F

Unit 4

C. 1. F 2. T 3. T 4. F 5. T 6. F 7. T 8. T 9. F 10. T

D. 1. hungry 2. sweet 3. refrigerator 4. prepared 5. bake 6. stove 7. prefer 8. lid, boils 9. potatoes

E. 1. their mother was sick 2. their father 3. He boiled them. 4. to buy potatoes 5. She took the meat out of the refrigerator, put salt on it, and put it in the oven to bake. 6. Mary 7. cake 8. everyone

Unit 5

C. 1. F 2. F 3. T 4. F 5. T 6. F 7. F 8. F 9. T

D. 1. The wedding will be next December.   2. Twins may look the same. 3. The young couple across the street got a divorce.   4. The anniversary was a time of great joy.   5. Friends and members of the family came to the party after the wedding./After the wedding, friends and members of the family came to the party.   6. She's pregnant for the fourth time.   7. Many of my relatives are divorced.   8. My nephew is very ambitious.

E. I. 1. g 2. h 3. c 4. a 5. f
II. 1. e 2. a 3. c 4. g

F. 1. at a young age 2. Many of them did not.   3. She did not marry young, and she stayed married.   4. go to weddings 5. She was very busy and seemed to be happy to spend time with her relatives.   6. at a wedding 7. She didn't have much time for her relatives, and she didn't like to go to weddings anymore.   8. not until her sons get married

Unit 6

C. 1. F 2. F 3. T 4. T 5. F 6. F 7. T 8. F 9. T 10. F

D. 1. patient 2. rest 3. rest 4. blanket 5. cure 6. medicine

E. 1. dentist 2. x-ray 3. condition 4. injury 5. exercise 6. die 7. blanket 8. blind 9. teeth 10. patients 11. fee 12. cure

Unit 7

C. 1. T 2. T 3. F 4. T 5. F 6. T 7. F 8. F 9. T 10. F

D. 1. locked 2. attacked 3. investigating, robbery 4. judge, robber 5. victim 6. lying 7. investigation

E. 1. broke the lock on the back door 2. They worked so silently. 3. many valuable things 4. three 5. Avoid leaving the house dark at night, and lock all doors and windows. 6. arrested them.

Unit 8

C. 1. defend 2. rank 3. surrender 4. guy 5. rank 6. above

D. 1. bomb, sank 2. marched 3. rank 4. surrendered 5. guys 6. above
7. command/control 8. destroyed/damaged 9. defend

E. 1. bombs from the enemy planes 2. the air force 3. sailing in the waters
near the coast 4. the army officers 5. late afternoon

Unit 9

C. 1. F 1. F 3. F 4. T 5. T 6. F 7. T 8. F 9. F 10. T 11. T 12. F
13. T 14. F

D. 1. brick 2. cotton 3. none 4. sell 5. never 6. common 7. cloth

E. 1. Cotton is appropriate material for summer clothes. 2. This wide belt was a
bargain. 3. My habitual breakfast is juice, bread, and cheese. 4. Several types
of insects came to our picnic. 5. I bought a thick, wool jacket for the
winter. 6. The clerk charged me too much for this shirt. 7. I don't like to
wear tight shoes. 8. That wide refrigerator won't fit into my small kitchen.
9. When I went to the beach, I lost my socks and sweater.

Unit 10

C. 1. b 2. d 3. a 4. c

D. 1. d 2. a 3. b 4. c

E. 1. T 2. F 3. F 4. T 5. T 6. F 7. T 8. T

F. 1. center 2. engines 3. lead, accident 4. loud 5. modern 6. instead
7. happened 8. narrow 9. leader

G. 1. F 2. F 3. T 4. T 5. F 6. T

Unit 11

C. 1. inform 2. symbolize 3. official 4. responsible 5. ordered 6. wished
7. vote 8. democracy 9. general 10. comments 11. international
12. capital 13. According

D. 1. about 2. for/on 3. on/about 4. for

E. 1. last year 2. every six years 3. no 4. in the capital city 5. the president's
promise to help all of the country

Unit 12

C. 1. T 2. T 3. F 4. T 5. F 6. F 7. F 8. F 9. F 10. F

D. 1. I put my money in an account. 2. He earns $3,000 each month. 3. They
carefully counted my money at the bank. 4. I get interest each month from
that account. 5. They borrowed money from a bank. 6. The exact total in
my account is $1,200.

E. 1. open a bank account 2. no 3. cash 4. people who have accounts with
them. 5. to find out which ones paid the highest interest. 6. (1). They paid
high interest. (2). They had a special type of account for university students.

Unit 13

C. **1.** agriculture **2.** rural **3.** seeds **4.** hay **5.** excess **6.** flood **7.** Peasants **8.** lack **9.** purpose **7.** share

D. **1.** cattle **2.** crop **3.** century **4.** flood **5.** crop **6.** flood

E. ACROSS: **1.** peasant **3.** crop **4.** excess **5.** lack **7.** seed **9.** farming **10.** supply **12.** share
DOWN: **1.** purpose **2.** agriculture **6.** century **8.** hay **9.** flood **11.** cattle

F. **1.** nothing but farms, two centuries ago **2.** corn, wheat, and other crops **3.** sold the excess in the local markets **4.** meat **5.** corn and hay

Unit 14

C. **1.** F **2.** F **3.** T **4.** T **5.** T **6.** T **7.** F **8.** T **9.** F **10.** F

D. **1.** A good basketball game is exciting. **2.** Some people play soccer indoors. **3.** They won the game because of their superior strength. **4.** She jumped high to get the ball. **5.** They are certain to win this game. **6.** He scored in the soccer game. **7.** The final score of this exciting contest was 66 to 65.

E. **1.** talent **2.** individual **3.** superior **4.** team **5.** fall **6.** weak **7.** natural

F. **1.** any time of year, indoors or outdoors. **2.** Both use a large ball, are played on a field or floor, and are fast-moving. Both score by putting the ball into the other team's defended area. **3.** with your hands, with your feet or another part of your body **4.** It is necessary to jump high and throw the ball high.

Unit 15

C. **1.** F **2.** F **3.** T **4.** F **5.** T **6.** F **7.** T **8.** T **9.** T **10.** F **11.** F

D. **1.** thermometer **2.** typical **3.** equator **4.** degrees **5.** freeze **6.** melt **7.** Perhaps **8.** measures **9.** under **10.** liquids **11.** gas

E. **1.** at the equator **2.** because of the heat **3.** if he had crossed the equator before **4.** It was a typical "party" for people crossing the equator for the first time.

Unit 16

C. **1.** T **2.** F **3.** F **4.** F **5.** T **6.** T **7.** F **8.** T **9.** T **10.** F **11.** T **12.** T

D. **1.** e **2.** c **3.** g **4.** a **5.** d **6.** b **7.** h **8.** f

E. **1.** oil **2.** the water and coastal areas **3.** They said they had invented a method to clean up floating oil. **4.** because the result of such oil leaks is major environmental pollution **5.** The oil reached the beaches. **6.** the deaths of many birds and fish

Unit 17

C. **1.** F **2.** T **3.** T **4.** T **5.** F **6.** T **7.** F **8.** F **9.** F **10.** F **11.** T **12.** T

D. **1.** print/publish **2.** title **3.** translator **4.** believed **5.** fact **6.** advertisement **7.** publish/print **8.** paragraphs

E. **1.** article **2.** entitle **3.** translation **4.** media **5.** question **6.** fact

F. **1.** author **2.** the media **3.** no **4.** because they forget that not everything that is published is factual **5.** <u>The Modern Media</u> ; yes **6.** The interview with Ackerman was very interesting.

Unit 18

C. **1.** F **2.** T **3.** T **4.** T **5.** F **6.** T **7.** F **8.** T

D. **1.** b **2.** a **3.** f **4.** j **5.** d **6.** h **7.** c **8.** i

E. **1.** discover/explore **2.** explore/discover **3.** path **4.** leafy **5.** pond **6.** rock **7.** snake **8.** afraid/fearful

Unit 19

C. **1.** T **2.** F **3.** F **4.** F **5.** T **6.** F **7.** T **8.** F

D. **1.** junior **2.** intelligent **3.** basic **4.** majored **5.** biology, chemistry **6.** incorrect **7.** history **8.** seat

E. **1.** John went to Peru during his junior year. **2.** The official spelled my name incorrectly. **3.** I wanted to study engineering. **4.** I don't like mathematics. **5.** My parents like to watch historical programs on TV. **6.** Chemistry was his undergraduate major. **7.** Susan wants to be a biologist.

F. **1.** science **2.** science, history, art, mathematics, chemistry, and biology **3.** She was intelligent and put a lot of effort into her homework. **4.** It allowed her to study both chemistry and engineering. **5.** the basics of engineering **6.** during her senior year

Unit 20

C. **1.** F **2.** T **3.** T **4.** F **5.** F **6.** T **7.** T **8.** F **9.** F **10.** F

D. **1.** efficient **2.** expert **3.** trains **4.** unemployed **5.** quit **6.** cooperate **7.** obvious **8.** similar **9.** certain **10.** tool

E. **1.** an expert **2.** It was producing ten buses a day instead of fifteen. **3.** He had been trained to study factories and help them be more efficient. **4.** other factory owners **5.** Many workers had quit during the last year. **6.** training in how to cooperate with other workers

Unit 21

C. **1.** T **2.** F **3.** F **4.** F **5.** T **6.** T **7.** T **8.** T **9.** T **10.** F

D. **1.** The price is reduced by 50%. **2.** This object is not for sale. **3.** The original price was $5. **4.** You can order this television from the factory. **5.** I saved a hundred dollars on the deal. **6.** We read the sign in the window. **7.** The company guarantees all its products.

E. **1.** originally **2.** sign **3.** inferior **4.** guarantee **5.** save **6.** valuable **7.** of course

F. **1.** a typewriter, winter clothing, television, or a used car **2.** by reading books and advertisements **3.** quality **4.** A poor quality product could be expensive, and a valuable one could be on sale at a greatly reduced price. **5.** The product may go on sale. **6.** 10, 20, or 50 percent off the original price **7.** You can get your money back if you don't like the product.

Unit 22

C. 1. F 2. T 3. F 4. F 5. T 6. T 7. F 8. F 9. F 10. T

D. 1. adapt 2. lonely 3. hesitant 4. imitate 5. previously 6. face 7. relax

E. 1. a. language b. food c. clothing 2. Don't hesitate to try it. 3. relaxing and pleasant 4. Visit some ancient buildings or museums. 5. approximately two or three hours

Unit 23

C. 1. F 2. F 3. T 4. T 5. F 6. F 7. T 8. T 9. F 10. T 11. F

D. 1. imagine 2. variety 3. sound 4. dramatic/ballet/theatrical 5. ballet 6. performance 7. entertainment 8. form 9. stare 10. actress

E. 1. to visit London, England 2. in a hotel in the theater area 3. took several long walks through the city, staring at all the famous buildings 4. a comedy by Tom Stoppard 5. a performance of <u>Swan Lake</u> 6. when she went to see <u>King Lear</u>

Unit 24

C. 1. F 2. F 3. T 4. T 5. F 6. F 7. T 8. T 9. F 10. T 11. F 12. T

D. 1. experiment 2. system 3. physics 4. determines 5. curious 6. complex 7. secret 8. dropped 9. astronomy 10. data 11. logical 12. collecting

E. 1. secret 2. boring 3. clear 4. calendar 5. democracy 6. destroy

F. 1. physicist 2. topics related to gravity 3. His government is afraid its enemies will steal the data. 4. He works systematically, plans experiments carefully, writes data clearly, repeats experiments, and tries to think of a logical explanation. 5. some exciting discoveries 6. a power related to gravity

Unit 25

C. 1. F 2. T 3. F 4. T 5. F 6. T 7. T 8. F 9. F 10. T

D. 1. manager 2. idea 3. closet 4. repair 5. shelf 6. sink 7. cabin 8. roof 9. downstairs 10. Avenue

E. 1. park 2. cabin 3. repair 4. preferable 5. work 6. basement 7. office 8. complaint 9. manager

F. 1. in dormitories, houses, and apartments 2. one year 3. a. Is it large enough? b. Is it convenient? c. Does it have enough furniture? Are there a stove and refrigerator? d. Is it quiet? e. Is there a place to park? f. What must I do if something goes wrong in the apartment?

Words Assumed for Volume 1

a
able
about
absent
after
again
age
ago
air
all
almost
already
also
always
an
and
animal
another
answer
any
anybody
anyone
anything
anywhere
apple
April
are
arm
arms
arrive
as
ask

at
August
aunt

baby
bad
ball
bank
bath
be (am, is,
   are, was,
   were, been)
beautiful
because
become
bed
before
begin
beside
best
better
between
big
bird
black
blackboard
blood
blue
board
boat
bone

book
born
both
box
boy
bread
breakfast
bring
brother
brown
build
   (built)
busy
but
buy
   (bought)
by

call
can
can't
car
cat
centimeter
chair
chicken
child
   (children)
church
city
class

clean
clock
clothes
clothing
coat
coffee
cold
color
come
complete
continue
cook
corner
correct
cost
could
country
cousin
cow
cry
cup
cut

dance
dark
daughter
day
dead
December
desk
different

difficult
dinner
dirty
do
doctor
dog
dollar
door
dormitory
down
dream
drink
drive
during

each
ear
east
easy
eat
egg
eight
elephant
eleven
end
enough
enter
etc. (etcetera)
every
explain
eye

February	gram	it	man (men)	no one
Friday	grandfather	its	many	(no-one)
face	grandmother	itself	map	north
fall (n)	grass		marry	nose
false	green		may	not
family		job	maybe	nothing
famous			me	now
far	hair		mean (v)	nowhere
fast	half	key	meat	number
fat	hand	kilogram	medicine	
father	handsome	kilometer	meet	
feel	happy	king	meter	ocean
feet	hat	kiss	might	o'clock
female	have	kitchen	milk	of
few	have to	knife	million	off
fifth	he	know	minute	office
find	head		mistake	often
fine	hear		money	old
finger	help	lady	month	on
finish	her	land	moon	once
fire	herself	language	more	one
first	here	large	morning	only
fish	high	last (adj)	most	open
five	him	late	mother	or
flag	himself	laugh	mountain	other
floor	his	learn	mouth	our
flower	hit	left	move	ours
fly	hold	leg	movies	ourselves
food	holiday	lesson	much	out
foot	home	letter	music	over
(feet)	hope	library	must	
forget	horse	life	my	
forth	hospital	like	myself	page
forty	hot	listen		paper
four	hotel	little		parent
free	hour	live	name	part
friend	house	long	near	party
from	how	look	necessary	past
front	hundred	a lot of	need	pay
fruit	husband	love	neighbor	peace
future		lunch	never	pen
			new	pencil
	I		news	permit
garden	ice	Miss	newspaper	person
get	idea	Mr.	next	(people)
gift	if	Mrs.	nice	picture
girl	important	machine	night	plane
give	in	magazine	nine	play
go	inside	mail	no	please
gold	interest	make	nobody	police
good	into	(made)	noise	poor
good-bye	is	male	none	practice

pretty	ship	stand	this	warm
price	shirt	start	those	wash
problem	shoe	stone	thousand	watch
put	shop	stop	three	water
	short	story	throw	way
	should	street	time	we
queen	show	strong	today	weather
question	shut	student	tomorrow	week
quiet	sick	study	tonight	well
	side	subject	too	west
	sing	such	tooth	what
radio	sister	sugar	top	when
railroad	sit	summer	train	where
rain	six	sun	tree	which
read	sleep	swim	true	white
red	slow		try	who
remember	small		twelve	whom
repeat	smile	table	twenty	why
return	snow	take	twice	wife
rice	so	talk	two	will
rich	soap	tall	type	winter
right	some	tea		with
river	somebody	teach		woman
road	somehow	telephone	umbrella	(women)
room	someone	tell	uncle	word
round	something	ten	understand	work
run	sometimes	test	university	would
	somewhere	thank	up	write
	son	the	us	wrong
sad	song	their	use	
salt	soon	them		
same	sorry	themselves		year
say	soup	then	very	yellow
school	south	therefore		yes
second	speak	these		yesterday
see	spell	they	wait	you
sell	spend	thin	wake	young
send	spoon	thing	walk	your
seven	sport	think	wall	yourself
she	spring	third	want	yourselves

In addition, the following closed sets have been assumed:

days of the week
months of the year
cardinal numbers
ordinal numbers

APPENDIX
C

Words in Volume 1

Numbers refer to **volume** and unit.

accept, **1-1**
address, **1-6**
advantage, **1-12**
afternoon, **1-15**
air force, **1-18**
airplane, **1-2**
airport, **1-2**
allow, **1-8**
ambition, **1-14**
ambulance, **1-16**
apartment, **1-3**
apply, **1-1**
army, **1-18**
around, **1-19**
artist, **1-14**
assign(ment), **1-8**
attempt, **1-1**
audience, **1-9**
automobile, **1-2**

back, **1-16**
bacon, **1-15**
band, **1-25**
barn, **1-19**
baseball, **1-10**
basement, **1-12**
beach, **1-9**
beef, **1-15**
bell, **1-8**

bench, **1-9**
bicycle, **1-11**
bill, **1-24**
bleed/blood, **1-16**
blow, **1-4**
body, **1-16**
boot, **1-17**
boring, **1-9**
boss, **1-5**
bowl, **1-15**
break, **1-16**
brick, **1-12**
bridge, **1-11**
bus, **1-2**
business, **1-5**

cafeteria, **1-8**
camera, **1-7**
camp, **1-21**
campus, **1-8**
card, **1-21**
careful/less, **1-5**
carry, **1-7**
cave, **1-21**
cent, **1-6**
chair, **1-12**
change, **1-17**
chapter, **1-8**
cheap, **1-6**

cheese, **1-15**
choose, **1-8**
clear, **1-4**
clerk, **1-6**
climb, **1-21**
coast, **1-23**
collect (call), **1-24**
college, **1-1**
comedy, **1-25**
comfortable, **1-12**
commit, **1-22**
common, **1-16**
communicate, **1-6**
company, **1-5**
compete, **1-10**
complete, **1-1**
concert, **1-9**
contract, **1-14**
cool, **1-21**
corn, **1-19**
cost, **1-21**
course, **1-8**
crime, **1-22**
cross, **1-11**
crowd, **1-10**

date, **1-21**
decide, **1-3**
declare, **1-20**

deep/depth, 1-23
deliver, **1**-6
dial, **1**-24
direction, **1**-21
dissappear, **1**-22
distance (long), 1-24
dormitory, 1-1
dress, 1-17
dry, **1**-4
dull, 1-25

early, **1**-4
earth, 1-23
edge, **1**-11
electricity, 1-3
elementary school, 1-1
else, 1-25
embassy/ambassador, 1-20
emergency, 1-24
employ(ee), 1-5
empty, **1**-2
enemy, 1-18
enjoy, 1-7
entertainment, 1-9
envelope, 1-6
ever, **1**-21
examine, 1-16
excited, 1-7
excuse, 1-16
expensive, 1-6
experience, 1-14

factory, 1-5
fan, 1-10
fan, 1-23
farm, 1-19
fear, 1-22
fence, 1-19
fever, 1-16
field, 1-19
fight, 1-18
film, 1-25
finally, 1-13
fog, **1**-23
forbid, 1-20
force, 1-20
forecast, 1-4
foreign, 1-6
fork, 1-15
fortunately, 1-14

frequent, 1-24
fresh, 1-15
frighten, 1-18
fun, 1-25
funny, 1-9
furniture, 1-3

game, 1-10
garage, **1**-12
gas, **1**-12
geography, 1-23
glad, **1**-7
glass, **1**-15
gloves, 1-17
golf, **1**-9
government, 1-20
grade, **1**-8
graduate, 1-1
ground, 1-23
group, 1-10
grow, 1-19
guard, 1-18
guess, 1-13
guest, 1-12
gun, 1-18

handle, 1-20
hang up, **1**-24
hard, 1-23
hate, 1-22
head, 1-20
health, 1-16
heat, 1-12
heavy, 1-13
helicopter, 1-18
high school, 1-1
hill, 1-23
hobby, 1-9
honest/honor, 1-20
horn, 1-11
horrible, 1-18
hurry, 1-11
hurt, 1-16

ill, 1-16
impersonal, 1-24
indoors, 1-10
insect, 1-21
instrument, 1-24

insure, 1-13
intersection, 1-11
interview, 1-5
invitation, 1-13
item, 1-13

jacket, 1-17
jail, **1**-22
joke, 1-25
juice, 1-15
jungle, 1-23

kill, **1**-18

landlord/lady, 1-3
lane, **1**-11
last (v), **1**-7
lawn, 1-12
lawyer, 1-14
lease, 1-12
leather, 1-17
leave, 1-7
license, 1-14
light, 1-13
light, 1-3
limit, 1-13
lobby, **1**-21
local, 1-24
lose/loss, 1-10
low, 1-14
luggage, 1-7

maid, **1**-14
message, 1-24
middle, **1**-11
midnight, 1-22
military, 1-18
mirror, 1-17
motel, 1-7
move, 1-11
mud, 1-23
murder, 1-22
mystery, 1-22

navy, 1-18
neighborhood, **1**-3
noon, 1-8
nurse, 1-14

Index

Words in Volume 2

Numbers refer to **volume** and unit.